Beyond

THE
LITTLE
MAC
BOOK

MW00682314

Beyond

THE
LITTLE
MAC
BOOK

Steve Broback
and Robin Williams

Peachpit Press
Berkeley * California

Beyond

The Little Mac Book

Steve Broback and Robin Williams
Copyright ©1997 Steve Broback and Robin Williams
Cover art by TMA Ted Mader Associates, Inc.
Clip art throughout book by Dean Stanton,
    the Hoopla Collection, available from Image Club
Interior design and production by Robin Williams
Edited by Robin Williams, Nancy Davis, and Jenifer Blakemore
Robin's hat in the photo is a gift from a dear, dear friend, Amanda Reckonwith

Peachpit Press

2414 Sixth Street
Berkeley, California 94710
510.548.4393
510.548.5991 fax

Find us on the World Wide Web at http://www.peachpit.com

Peachpit Press is a division of Addison Wesley Longman

Notice of Rights

All rights reserved. No part of this book may be reproduced or transmitted in any form or by any means, electronic, mechanical, photocopying, recording, or otherwise, without the prior written permission of the publisher.

For information on obtaining permission for reprints and excerpts, contact Trish Booth at Peachpit Press.

Notice of Liability

The information in this book is distributed on an "as is" basis, without warranty. While every precaution has been taken in the preparation of this book, neither the authors nor Peachpit Press shall have any liability to any person or entity with respect to any liability, loss, or damage caused or alleged to be caused directly or indirectly by the instructions contained in this book or by the computer software and hardware products described herein.

Trademarks

Throughout this book trademarked names are used. Rather than put a trademark symbol in every occurrence of a trademarked name, we state we are using the names only in an editorial fashion and to the benefit of the trademark owner with no intention of infringement of the trademark.

ISBN

0-201-88666-9

10 9 8 7 6 5 4 3

Printed and bound in the United States of America

To Vicky
With all my love
and appreciation.
Steve

Hey Steve, this one's for you!
Thanks ever so much,
Robin

Thanks ever so much!

To Robin Williams for asking me to work on this book, and being a wonderful partner in its conception and production. To Steve Roth who introduced me to the folks at Peachpit, and has given me a terrific amount of support during this project. To David Hoffman for his confidence and guidance. To the patient folks at Peachpit Press, specifically Ted Nace for bringing me on board, and Nancy Davis who drove this book forward while being a joy to work with at the same time. To the gang who helped put it all together: Agen Schmitz, Jeff Carlson, and Myke Ninness. To my beta test team—the people I wrote this book for: Julie Myers, David Lake, and LeRoy Kuebler. To my coworkers, for their patience, support, and use of their Macs after-hours: Toby Malina, Krista Carriero, Michele Dionne, Sondra Wells, Dom Prandini, Ole Kvern, and David Blatner. To my family: Vicky, John, and Nancy Broback, and my little hoodlums Dalton and Emma, who gave up many a Saturday morning with their daddy to make this book possible. *Steve*

Nancy Davis, you went far beyond the call of duty on this one! I enjoy working with you so much. Jenifer Blakemore and Stephanie van Dyck—I couldn't have gotten it done in time without you. Kate Reber, you're great. John Tollett, I adore you. Jimmy Thomas and Scarlett Williams, thanks for making dinners and going grocery shopping. Ryan, I miss you. And Steve Broback, you done good. It was truly a great treat working with you. *Robin*

Contents

1   Know the Hardware   17

2   Master Your System Folder   41

Foreword, from Robin

When I originally self-published *The Little Mac Book,* it *was* a little book, only 102 pages. The book has gotten bigger because, alas, the Mac has gotten bigger. And now the information spills into a second volume.

Ted Nace, former publisher of Peachpit Press, suggested this book. I didn't want to do it because I knew there would have to be a lot of stuff about hardware and troubleshooting and what to clean out of your System Folder. I'm a teacher, not a consultant or a technical support person. So one day at the end of a ThunderLizard PageMaker conference, I was talking with Steve Broback. Steve is a brilliant guy, he is one of the best public speakers I have ever heard, he is amazingly knowledgeable about Macs, he is a wonderful teacher, and he is a consultant and a tech support sort of person. He knows all that stuff about hardware and troubleshooting and what to clean out of your System Folder. He's worked with thousands of Macs and their owners over the years. Aha—he was the perfect person to write this book. A year or so later, here it is, and he did a great job. Steve wrote the book (so don't get confused when he mentions "my wife"); I edited, added my two cents here and there, and designed and produced the book. As a teacher, I'm a firm believer that how the words are presented on the page are as important to a person's understanding as what they say.

When I teach, I don't provide all the answers at once. I usually wait until a student has the problem, then I explain the solution. I have to hold my tongue sometimes, but I have learned that, very often, the solution doesn't make sense until you've had the problem. That is the purpose of this book—you've been working with your Mac for a while and you've bumped into some problems. You're ready for the answers now, and Steve has them for you.

Robin Williams

Introduction, from Steve

Apple's original vision for the Macintosh was an easy-to-use, cute, minimalist, little machine that could handle all the computing needs of the average person. Its informal, laid-back style was attractive to anyone who just wanted to get their work done without turning computing into a major hobby. It really was "the computer for the rest of us."

Surprisingly, for a long time, the books published for Mac users did not follow the formula that made the Mac itself so popular. Dry, and far from minimalist, they followed the tried-and-true computer book formula—plenty of long-winded jargon. Things changed dramatically in 1989 when the original *Little Mac Book* hit the bookstores. Like the Mac itself, *The Little Mac Book* was cute, small, uncluttered, and as an added bonus, it "talked" the way real people do. Robin Williams' approach was so well received it spawned an entire genre of how-to computer books—light in tone and not mired in detail. Years after its debut, *The Little Mac Book* remains the best choice to gently lead new users to Mac competence.

The Mac has improved a lot since 1984 when those first little computers were criticized for their lack of a hard disk, inadequate RAM, and tiny screen. So has the IBM PC. We Mac users have been vindicated over time as innovations like the mouse, the trash can, and "plug and play" have been accepted by almost all computer users. No longer are we laughed at by the macho DOS users who are now using a mouse and trash can—I mean, recycle bin.

The Mac of today can rightfully claim the title of most powerful personal computer available. No other machine can run DOS, Windows, Mac, and Unix software simultaneously. The implementation of RISC technology has provided us with one of the most powerful CPU chips on the desktop. No other computer enthralls the true "power users" like the Mac.

The problem is: The Mac has grown into a complex machine that in most ways has outgrown its "computer for the rest of us" theme. The simple little "information appliance" of 1984 has become a multi-headed hydra of Extension programs, Enabler software, and 20-megabyte word processors. It is for this reason that we decided to do a follow-up to the original *Little Mac Book*. Our goal was to provide a way for the basic Mac user to move to "power user" status without having to wade through the minutiae that clogs up so many of those 800-page books on the shelves today.

So, here it is.

Know the Hardware

1

What You Don't Need to Know

Remember when you decided to get into computers? Maybe you needed to make a career change, wanted to simplify your finances, or just thought it sounded fun.

Whatever your reason, you may have thought you had to know how the hardware worked. This was one of my first (of many) computer learning mistakes. I started reading books about how the binary system of counting works, how a processor chip can act as a set of electronic switches, and what physically happens in RAM.

Not only did all that stuff make my head swim (I never did get it), but it was like trying to learn the physics of gasoline combustion in order to drive a car! What a relief it was to discover that knowing the intricacies of how the hardware works is totally unnecessary to becoming adept at using a computer.

So you're asking, "Then why a chapter on hardware?" Here's the reason—you don't need to know *how* these components work. You need to know *what they do*. Why does my favorite program run great one day and another day it won't even launch? Why does program X run so slow? Does installing an accelerator board make sense? Will the new software I'm considering buying run on my System? Should I buy that used machine? These are the types of questions that a little hardware savvy can answer.

Processors

Understanding the Mac's processor, or CPU chip (central processing unit) is the place to start. This is the most important component and is really the heart of the computer. In the beginning, Apple used the Motorola 68000 family of processors. They had several advantages over the Intel X86 family that IBM PC's and compatibles used—the main one being their superiority in handling graphics. I'm sure there were some politics involved as well—I doubt that Apple would have used Intel's chip in any circumstance, since IBM owned about ten percent of Intel when the Mac was being designed.

The **68000** was the original Mac processor chip. It was a speed demon for its time, but of course it's considered a slug today. You can find this chip in the Mac 128, 512, Plus, SE, Classic, Macintosh Portable, and PowerBook 100. Very few programs being developed today will run on a 68000 machine.

The **68020** was introduced in 1987 and was significantly faster. Apple installed it in the MacII and the LC. Many of the latest software programs will run (very slowly) on 68020 machines .

68030 chips were faster still, and Macs like the SE 30, Classic 2, IIci, IIcx, IIsi, LCII, FX, LC 550, and PowerBooks 150, 160, 170, and 180 use it. They're great for some home applications (games, ClarisWorks, etc.) and very basic publishing work.

68040 is the last of the 68000 family of chips that Apple is using. If you have an LCIII, anything named Quadra or Centris, or a Power-Book 520, 540, or 550, this is the "brain" inside your machine.

There is a "dumbed-down" version of the 68040 chip, called the **68LC040,** which is missing the internal math coprocessor. Since few programs ever took advantage of this feature, most owners of those chips never notice its absence. The majority of the Mac models using the '040 chip are using this less expensive chip.

Apple made a dramatic move in 1991. They decided to go to a totally new type of processor. The reason? They were getting clobbered in the marketplace by the IBM-compatibles with the **Pentium** chips. The Pentium machines were not only cheaper (Macs had always been more expensive), but they were noticeably faster. Apple's bread-and-butter (the design and imaging community) had started defecting to machines that could give them the speed they needed, so Apple needed a fast alternative.

Apple decided to go RISC.

68000 Family vs. PowerPC

You may remember a few years ago when Apple and IBM formed an alliance to develop new computer systems together—it was a big deal in the papers and on the news. The idea was that Apple would contribute their software and systems expertise while IBM had this new design for a super-processor that used **RISC** technology (Reduced Instruction Set Computing) that they could throw into the ring.

Together, they could develop a combination that might make a dent in the Intel/Microsoft juggernaut. They promised new computers that would be faster and cheaper than anything on the market.

They called these new processors **PowerPC** chips. If you have a Macintosh with a PowerPC chip inside, you have a **Power Mac.**

Power Macs use the PowerPC Chip.

RISC vs. CISC

RISC chips had been used in expensive scientific workstations for years. These types of chips have several big advantages over the traditional **CISC** (Complex Instruction Set Computing) chips. The biggest one is that they can process information using fewer instructions. Together with a manufacturing process that creates a smaller processor, they're also (theoretically) cheaper to build.

The downside? Putting a radically new type of chip in a computer means that all software has to be completely rewritten to run on it!

Imagine telling software developers to rewrite all their Mac programs for an untested new machine with unknown market viability—most would probably sit it out. So Apple came up with a solution.

68000 Emulation

Apple came up with a simple, elegant (although a little slow) solution. They built an **emulator chip** into their systems that would automatically kick in whenever the computer sensed you were trying to run an older 68000-based program. This emulator acted as a "pretend" 68040 chip so that your older software wouldn't freak out.

This allowed Apple to come to market very quickly with new machines that would run your old software. As the software companies created PowerPC versions of your favorite software, you could come up to speed gradually.

Today when you install software, you are often given the choice of installing a 68000 version, a PowerPC version, or a **"fat binary"** version, which includes both.

Software that has been written specifically for the PowerPC chip is called **native.** The 68000 programs run in **emulation** on Power Macs.

PowerPC

If you have a Macintosh with this logo
printed on the case, you have a Power Macintosh.

PowerPC Processor Choices

When you buy a Power Macintosh, it comes with one of six basic PowerPC chips:

The **601** was the first PowerPC chip, and the slowest of all. The original Power Macs came out with this chip.

The **603** chip came out soon after, and is really just a version of the 601 designed for portable devices like PowerBooks. It generates less heat and uses less electricity than the 601. It is actually slower than the 601. There are some newer versions of the 603 called the **603e** and the **603ev,** which are about as fast as the 601.

The **604** chip is the fastest. It is much faster than the 601 or the 603, and there is a new version of the 604 called the **604e,** which is the fastest PowerPC chip available at the moment.

Apple's promise of faster and cheaper Macintoshes hasn't quite happened yet. The new Macs are about as fast as their Pentium counterparts (chip-making engineers could have told us years ago that the whole RISC vs. CISC thing is silly—that it's possible to add RISC elements gradually to a CISC chip family). Intel has integrated RISC technology into the Pentium with some success.

What about cheaper? Hmmm . . . since Intel makes millions of Pentiums a year with lots of competitive pressures, it has been able to reduce chip costs greatly. PowerPC chips are produced in numbers one-tenth of that amount, and Apple/IBM/Motorola have no competition for that particular chip. Net result is that Pentium boxes still are a bit less expensive. But you get what you pay for.

Clock Speed

Even though the processor is the primary determinant of speed, there is another crucial element that also affects how fast you can get your work done. It is the processor's rated speed, usually called "clock speed." The clock speed is measured in **megahertz** (or MHz for short); the higher the MHz, the faster the chip. A PPC 601 at 60 MHz is slower than the same chip at 90 MHz.

Many people get obsessed about clock speed—they use it as the be all and end all of speed comparison (can you say "Windows users"?) They'll even compare two totally different chip families and say one's faster because of the clock speed. This is silly. A Zamster 9000 CPU chip at 100 MHz is not necessarily faster than a Liguana 80472 at 82 MHz. If that were true, then a 68000 chip at 33 MHz should be faster than a 68040 at 25 MHz, which is just plain silly!

Level Two Cache

A Power Mac may have something called a Level Two Cache, which is different from the regular cache in your Mac (page 78). Level Two Cache is a special type of fast RAM that acts as a middleman between your regular RAM and the processor chip. A Level Two Cache holds information that it thinks the processor may ask for soon. When the processor asks for data that's in the cache, the requested data gets zapped to the processor very, very, quickly—much faster than if the processor had to retrieve it from regular RAM. This means a significant speed improvement—as much as 38% over a Mac without one of these caches.

Coprocessors

In some of the earlier Macs (pre-68040 machines) Apple would throw in a special second processor to take some of the load off of the main CPU chip.

FPU

The **FPU** (or Floating Point Unit) was designed to speed up certain math operations. Eventually its functions were folded into the 68040 chip itself. Today, the PowerPC chip contains its own revamped version of this coprocessor.

PMMU

Another early coprocessor was the **PMMU** (Paged Memory Management Unit). The PMMU was a required component for a Mac to use 32-bit-addressing, which is a requirement if you want to use more than 8 megabytes of RAM on 68020 machines. All chips newer than the 68020 (the 68030, 68040, and PowerPC chips) have the PMMU component built in.

The Role of ROM

Most Mac users consider their System and Finder to be the two main programs in control of their computers. That's true, but you need to consider the System and Finder's silent partner, the **ROM** (Read-Only Memory) chip inside the Mac. You never actually see this chip. It sits inside your computer, quietly doing its job. Its read-only status means even if you could access it, you couldn't make changes to it anyway. This is why most Mac users aren't even aware it exists.

Think of this chip as the foundation that the System and Finder are built upon. This chip actually contains a significant amount of your operating system software (I can't really call it software, since it's on a chip—*firmware* is the correct term). Mac geeks sometimes refer to the ROM as the **Toolbox.** Much of your Mac's personality resides on this chip. Its ability to create on-screen windows, manipulate a mouse, or create pull-down menus is drawn from the Toolbox.

The Mac ROMs are the "crown jewels" of Apple. Think about it— what would you need to buy to start building your own Macintosh? Hard disks and RAM can be bought anywhere. Processor chips can be purchased directly from Motorola. Keyboards and mice are easy to come by. Put all that stuff together and you get a near worthless pile of components. (Hmm, you can build a PC in your kitchen.)

It's the ROMs that make a Mac a Mac! No one has yet been able to duplicate this chip, and that's why there are no Mac clones (except for those licensed from Apple). All Apple is basically doing when they license a clone manufacturer is letting them buy ROM chips!

Many consider this to be the Macintosh's main advantage over the Windows platform. Since much of the operating system (OS) is in ROM, less RAM is required for a graphical user interface. The fact that you can run the best desktop operating system today off of a **single floppy**—in less than 1400K—is very impressive compared to the RAM-hogging and disk-gobbling of Windows.

Different Macs have different ROMs. That's what makes each Mac model have its own distinct personality. The Mac Plus ROMs can use only 4 megabytes of RAM; most PowerBooks have ROMs that allow them to be used as external hard disks; the Mac Classic ROMs have a complete hidden System Folder within them! This is one reason I avoid buying an accelerator for an older Mac: sure, I can get an old machine to run faster, but software that is "seeing" a new processor and unexpected older ROMs can get confused and crash more often.

Memory

Although I advocate a minimalist Mac, the one area where more is always better is in regards to memory.

The RAM chips inside your Macintosh constitute your available workspace. The larger the workspace, the more programs you can run, and each can run more reliably. Each Mac has an upper limit for RAM expansion. As of this writing, the top model is the Power Mac 9600, which can take 768 MB. At the low end is the Mac Plus, SE and Classic, which top out at 4 MB.

How can you tell the upper limit on your machine? Here's a table of memory limits for just about every Mac ever made:

Macintosh Model	RAM Limit (in Megabytes)
Plus, SE, Classic	4
II, IIx	8
IIcx (pre–System 7)	8
IIcx (with Mode 32 or System 7)	128
Classic II, Color Classic, SE 30, LC, LC II	10
IIsi, Quadra 700	17
IIvi	20
IIci	32
LC III, LC 475, LC 520, LC 550, LC 575, LC 630, Quadra 605 and 630	36
LC 580, LC 630 (DOS Compatible), 5200/75 LC	52
Quadra 900, 5260/120, 6200/75	64
All 6100 models	72
IIfx, Centris/Quadra 610, Quadra/Centris 660AV	68
Quadra 840AV, 5500/225, all 6500 models	128
Quadra 650	132
Centris 650, Quadra 800, 6400/200, all 5400 and 7100 models	136
All 4400 models	160
Quadra 950, all 7200 and 8200 models	256
All 8100 models	264
all 7300, 7500, 7600, 8500 and 8600 models	512
all 9500 and 9600 models	768

Performas

Performa Model	RAM Limit
200, 250, 405, 410, 430	10
275, all 450–476 models, all 550–578 models, all 630–638 models	36
580CD, 630 (DOS Compatible) and 640CD (DOS Compatible)	52
all 5200–5320 models, all 6200–6360 models	64
600CD	68
6100CD	72
all 5400, 5420, and 6400 models	136

PowerBooks

PowerBook Model	RAM Limit
100, 140, 145, 145B, 170	8
160, 165, 165c, 180, 180c	14
Duo 210, Duo 230, Duo 250, Duo 270c	24
all 190 and 500 series models	36
all 150, 280, and 190 series models	40
Duo 2300c/100	56
all 1400 and 5300 series models	64
all 3400 models	144

Installing and Upgrading Memory

Most Macs come with a certain amount of memory soldered on the motherboard. This is usually a fixed amount and is essentially untouchable. Adding more RAM means plugging a **SIMM** or **DIMM** (Single/ Double Inline Memory Module, or memory chips) into a slot or series of slots on the motherboard reserved for this purpose. If you're lucky, your memory slots are currently unused and you can just plug in more chip(s). If not, adding RAM will mean removing existing SIMMs or DIMMs and putting in new, larger ones.

Here's an example: At home I have an LCII with 6 megabytes of RAM. I have 4 megabytes soldered onto the motherboard, and two SIMM slots. Each slot already has a one-megabyte SIMM in it. To upgrade the computer to 8 megabytes, I'd have to remove the one-megabyte SIMMs that are already installed and fill those two slots each with two-megabyte SIMMs.

Upgrading RAM usually requires opening the case to your Mac, finding the slots, and correctly inserting new RAM chips. Some mail-order houses will include videos showing how to install the RAM when you purchase it from them.

Parameter RAM: Preventing Ramnesia

The problem with RAM is that everything in it goes away when you shut off the computer—poof! But there are some things the Mac wants to remember without having to dredge them out of your hard disk. This is why we have **Parameter RAM,** or **PRAM** for short (pronounced "pee ram"). PRAM is a separate little RAM area that is maintained by a little battery inside your computer.

Stored in PRAM are many of your Control Panel settings, time, date, and various other tidbits of information. Many DOS computers require you to enter the date and time every time you start them up! The Mac was one of the first systems to bypass all this hassle by storing all that stuff in PRAM.

Monitors

It's easy to become overwhelmed when deciding on a new computer monitor. It wasn't long ago that you only had one choice on the Mac—the Sony 13-inch Trinitron screen with the Apple logo. It was a terrific (and expensive) monitor.

Today, you have dozens of options—monitors that double as TVs, screens that come with speakers and sound inputs embedded in them, and confusing buzzwords like "dot pitch" and "shadow masking" to worry about. Let's see what options are important, simplify the jargon, and decide how to get the most bang for the buck.

Generally, when comparing monitors, here are the things you want:

- A big screen (for seeing enough pixels)
- A flat screen (reduces glare and distortion)
- A sharp screen (small details are clearer and eyestrain is reduced)

Screen Size

Let's talk first about screen size. Most vendors describe screen size in inches. They'll say they have a 14-, 15-, or 17-inch monitor. This is a *diagonal measurement* across the tube, and it describes the size of the glass. If you look at a computer screen that's actually turned on, you'll notice there's a black ring of unused area, about a half-inch wide, surrounding the live area of the screen. Because of this unused area, Apple used to do the right thing and call their monitors 13 inches in size, when the actual glass was 14 inches across. Nobody else did, though, and a perception began that Apple's monitor wasn't as big as those typical in the DOS/Windows world. Apple finally gave in and now calls it a 14-inch display just like everybody else.

Another way to describe screen size is in **resolution,** or pixels, measuring how many pixels display across the screen by how many down (a pixel is one dot on the screen; there are usually around 72 pixels per inch). The usual configuration is **640 pixels** horizontally by **480 pixels** vertically. The typical 14-inch monitor made today is designed to be run at this resolution. Most games and multimedia programs are also designed with this resolution in mind. You've already discovered this if you own one of the early Macs with the cute little black-and-white screens. Since they're limited to 512 by 342, most games and multimedia CDs won't run on them.

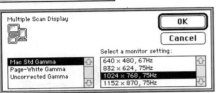

It may be possible for your 14-inch screen to show more pixels than 640 by 480. You can find out: open your Monitors Control Panel and click the "Options…" button. Even if you have this capability, you probably won't want to take advantage of the extra dots—you get *more* dots, but they're all *smaller* (it's like a bird's-eye view). You'll spend a lot of time squinting at those tiny pixels. Moving to a higher resolution like 800 by 600 is really only practical on a larger monitor, such as a 15-inch model. On really big screens you can get such resolutions as 1152 by 870.

Resolution is a relevant way to describe monitor size because it's a way to compare different brands. I heard a story a few years ago about some company selling a 17-inch screen that could only do 640 by 480! Sure, you got a bigger screen, but it didn't show any more infor-

These are the resolution options for Robin's 20-inch monitor. Notice she can't get "millions" of colors; the most she can see are "thousands." She needs to install separate VRAM to enable millions of colors to be sent to all those pixels on that huge monitor, or she needs to reduce the pixel count (resolution).

mation than an El Cheapo 14-inch model—the pixels were just bigger.

Most monitors bundled with computer systems are either 14 or 15 inches in glass size. My advice when shopping is to measure the actual active area of the screen, and ignore the numbers the manufacturers tout.

The monitors for sale today range from the standard 14-inch size up to 21 inches or more. I constantly get asked whether a large (16 inches or larger) monitor is worth the extra dollars, and for the typical user the answer is "No." The price difference between a 14- and 16-inch display is over $300, and jumping to 20 inches costs over $1,000 extra! I usually advise clients to buy more RAM or a faster processor. If you're a graphics or publishing professional, you can ignore my advice and decide for yourself.

I do not recommend saving even more money and going smaller than 14-inch, 640 by 480 (luckily, no new Mac or monitor comes smaller than this, just used machines) because much of the latest software won't run at a lower resolution.

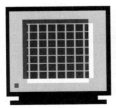

A smaller monitor may be able to show more data than a big monitor if it is set to a higher resolution.

Flat Screens

Flatter screens are better than really curvy ones for two reasons: it's easier to avoid glare off the monitor, and there's less distortion of what appears on screen. Just get up close and take a look. If you work in a particularly bright or harshly lit environment, glare becomes a big issue. In homes and offices without so much harsh light, having a more rounded display is not a big deal.

Sharp Image

If you really want to test how sharp a screen is, create some really small serif type like Times or New York (try 9-point size). Take a close look at the characters and see if there are small "rainbows" near the edges. The fuzzier the display, the more apparent this will be. Try the same thing with white type on a black background.

Another way to compare general sharpness is to find out if the monitor in question has a Trinitron or a Tridot tube. Trinitron is generally considered sharper. When comparing two Trinitron screens, ask about the **aperture pitch.** This is a fancy way of describing how fine the metal grille behind the phosphors is; smaller numbers are better. Tridot screens use **dot pitch** as their measurement, and again, smaller is better.

How Many Colors?

If you're using a Mac, you probably have a color monitor. The question is "How many colors are available to you?" The monitor itself doesn't really have a practical limit—the video data output from your computer is the gating item. What you need to know is what the limits of your system are and how you can improve the situation.

To find out what your system and monitor are capable of, open your Monitors Control Panel. Look at the number of colors available. If you're using a color monitor, you'll probably see a maximum choice of 256 colors. If you're lucky, your choices may go to thousands (32 thousand, actually), or as high as millions (16.7 million). The bit depth and VRAM explained on the following pages are two of the determining factors in the number of colors you can see on your monitor.

This Mac has only 512K of VRAM, which limits it to 256 colors on most monitors. Clicking the "Options" button may let you try different resolutions.

Bit Depth

Most of the Macintoshes built today have a connection in the back where you're supposed to plug in the display. This connection usually sends out enough data to project 256 colors on a typical screen. The computer experts refer to this as having **8-bit** color.

Larger screens (typically greater than 640 by 480) require more information output from the system and may not be capable of showing all 256 colors. If you have a big screen and don't seem to be getting all the colors you want, open up the Monitors Control Panel. Reduce your resolution to 640 by 480 pixels (this is the typical resolution of a 13- to 14-inch monitor). You should now be able to see 8-bit color.

If you want to really sound like a computer expert, you have to talk about **bit depth.** This is simply a techie way to indicate how many colors something is capable of showing. A bit is one tiny unit of information, the tiniest the computer can use, sometimes displayed as 1s and 0s (ones and zeros, binary). On a black-and-white monitor, it takes one bit of information to turn a pixel on or off, black or white. So with one bit of information, you get two colors: black and white. If a pixel is smart enough to understand two bits of information, it can display four different colors: both bits on, both bits off, one off one on, one on one off (two of the colors are always black and white). Thus a 4-bit machine, like the PowerBook 520, can display 16 colors because you can arrange those four bits of information in 16 different ways. And an 8-bit machine can display 256 colors

The very first Macintoshes were 1-bit machines. Their monitors could only show black and white. No grays, no color. Those prehistoric machines fooled your eyes into thinking they saw gray by alternating the black and white pixels; this is sometimes called **dithering.** Soon the Mac II came along, and its ROMs could support up to 24-bit color (16.7 million colors). At that time you had to add a special circuit board for video-out capability. The less expensive boards could support 8-bit color, while a more expensive 24-bit version was available for graphics professionals.

So, a standard Mac today has 8-bit color output as standard equipment. This is plenty for someone making pie charts in Excel or running most home and business software. A professional photographer needing to retouch color photos will find this terribly limiting. Graphics professionals will want to upgrade to 16-bit (32,000 colors) or more likely 24-bit (16.7 million) colors. To do this you need to upgrade part of your *computer,* not your *monitor!*

With only one bit of information sent to a pixel, the pixel can be only one of two things: on or off.

Four bits of information can be sent to a pixel in sixteen different ways to produce sixteen different colors.

VRAM

Most Macs can have minor surgery that will increase the number of colors available. Adding more video RAM (VRAM, pronounced "vee ram") is one answer. VRAM is a special type of memory chip that acts as the workspace for the video-out signal coming from the computer. The more VRAM installed, the more colors available.

Here is how installed VRAM relates to color depth on various monitors and resolutions.

VRAM:	512K	768K	1 MB	2 MB	4 MB
640 by 480 pixels	256	32,768	32,768	16.7 Million	16.7 Million
832 by 624 pixels	256	256	32,768	16.7 Million	16.7 Million
1024 by 768 pixels	16	256	256	32,768	16.7 Million
1152 by 870 pixels	16	16	256	32,768	16.7 Million

What's the story with your Mac? Can you upgrade your machine with more VRAM to get more colors? Here are some basic guidelines:

- Of all the Macs made since 1984, 31 cannot do color or have no inherent color video capability, so VRAM upgrading is impossible.
- Another 21 use DRAM (System memory) which also cannot be upgraded.
- Another 21 are not expandable beyond the 512K level.

Those that max out at 768K VRAM:

- The LCIII and any Mac with a 450, 460, 520, 550, or 560 in the name.

Those that max out at 1 Megabyte VRAM:

Macintosh: IIvi, IIvx.

Quadras (or **Centris**): 610, 650, 800, 605, and 660AV.

PowerBooks: 5300, 3400 series models, and all Duo Docks.

Performas: (or LC) 470, 570, 580, 600, 630, 640, 5200, 5300, 6200 series models, and the Performa 6300CD and 6320CD.

Power Macs: 6100 and 6200 series.

Workgroup Servers: 60 and 80.

Those that can't be expanded beyond 2 megabytes VRAM:

Quadras: 700, 900, 950, 840AV.

Performas: 5400CD, 5400/180 DE, and 5420CD.

Power Macs: all 7100 and 6100AV models.

Workgroup Servers: 95.

Those that max out at 4 megabytes VRAM:

Performas: 6360/160, and all 6400 models.

Power Macs: all can upgrade to 4 megabytes except the 6100, 7100, and 6200 series.

The **Power Mac** 7100 and 8100 (non-AV models) have two video-out ports as standard equipment; one port is connected to the motherboard, the other is attached to a plug-in board. The one on the motherboard uses DRAM and cannot be upgraded. The plug-in board contains upgradable VRAM. The card for the 7100 can go up to 2 megabytes, while the 8100's card will go to 4 megabytes.

Video Cards

If you have a Macintosh that cannot benefit from a VRAM upgrade, or if you're using a monitor that can display so many pixels that adding VRAM still won't give you all the colors you need, you may be able to install a video board that can solve the problem.

You've probably seen ads from companies like Radius that tout 24-bit color cards at prices anywhere from $350 to $1,000 or more. These cards not only can give you more bit depth, but often are accelerated so that the screen redraw is much zippier.

These cards go into a slot inside the computer itself, and provide a connector out the back for plugging your screen into. These cards plug into an expansion slot (see pages 36–37 for more info on slots).

Storage

You have to keep your stuff somewhere right? Well, no doubt you're currently saving your work onto the hard disk that came with your system. Sitting inside your computer is a rigid metal disk or several stacked platters that are housed inside an airtight metal box about the size of a paperback book. This disk or disks contain your main application programs and most of your work files. What more is there to know?

Plenty. All computer users at some time have to deal with one or more of the following:

- The hard disk that came with the computer has died.
- The hard disk that came with the computer is filled up.
- The hard disk that came with the computer is too slow.
- Floppy disks don't hold enough data for the tasks required.

Hard Disks

Let's say you've decided to buy a new hard disk for any of the reasons listed above. What do you need to consider?

Assuming you have decided to get a newer, larger main hard disk (one of the first three reasons above), you'll need to decide between an external or internal disk. An internal disk goes inside the computer, while an external disk is in a separate box that plugs into the back of your Mac with a cable.

External hard disks

Many people like using an external model. They're easy to install. If they break, you can easily remove them so the disk can get fixed without having to take your computer into the shop as well. Also, you can easily relocate external hard disks—take your hard disk from your office to your home so you can work on it there.

There are a few problems: External hard disks take up desk space. It's one more cable to worry about. It makes moving your entire computer more of a hassle. My solution is to use an internal hard disk as my main disk and external hard disks as backups and for extra storage.

Removable Storage

You're set—you have a big, fast hard disk that holds all your work and applications. You now have a place to store all your stuff right? Wrong.

The problem with computers today is that the applications people run tend to create larger files than in the old days (all those graphics!). With all this storage, we also create more documents. The combination of more and significantly larger files, in tandem with floppy disks remaining the same tiny size since 1987, has spawned an entire industry of removable storage devices. Now backing up and transporting data is done less and less on floppy disks, and more and more on special disks and tapes.

Tape backup and storage

For years you've been able to buy small boxes that plug in to the SCSI port in the back of the computer that accept special tapes for computer data. Today the most popular kind of tape drives are called **DAT** (Digital Audio Tape) drives and run about $700 per device. The tapes are about $10 apiece and hold anywhere from two to eight gigabytes of information. These drives are about the most cost effective way to archive or transport large amounts of data.

There are a couple of real limitations to DAT tapes. One is that to find a certain piece of information, you have to rewind through all the other information. Also, they are not designed for a lot of use, for many reads and writes to the tape. For these reasons, DAT tapes are most often used for archiving, backing up, and for restoring entire hard disks.

Zip and Syquest drives

For a long time, if you wanted some kind of sizable external storage medium that also had decent access speeds, you were pretty much forced to buy a Syquest drive. Your only other choices were Magneto Optical disks and drives (mega-expensive) and traditional Bernoulli disks and drives (also mega-expensive).

The Syquest company doesn't make the drive mechanism itself; they just license the plans and rights to other drive manufacturers. What Syquest does make are the cartridges themselves—hard disk platters inside a plastic shell. Sounds like they learned one of the first lessons of business: give away the razors and sell the blades!

Syquest drives originally cost around $700, had cartridges that held 44 megabytes, and the cartridges cost about $60. Over several years the price dropped to about $400 per device, and the drives could use 270-megabyte cartridges that ran $70 apiece—not exactly cheap. On top of this, the traditional cartridges are really bulky (about the size of a big paperback book).

Then the **Zip drive** came along. In mid 1995 the folks from Iomega suddenly came to market with a $199 device that had $20 cartridges! Although the cartridges held "only" 100 megabytes, they were floppy sized. Finally—cheap, compact, and fast data storage. People started buying them like crazy, and Bernoulli stock went through the roof.

A few weeks after Zip drives came out, Syquest came out with their **EZ** model—an inexpensive smaller drive that uses compact, cheap disks! Many people thought Syquest was milking the market for as long as it could with a bulky, overpriced (not to mention noisy) device while they had this better, cheaper drive waiting in the wings.

Buying a hard disk

Buying a good hard disk is really pretty simple these days. They're cheap, more reliable than ever, and fast. It used to be we worried a lot about obscure and difficult terms like "access time" and "transfer rate" which describe the performance of a hard disk mechanism. This is pretty much a non-issue today.

Expandability—Slots and SCSI

Expansion Slots

The original Mac, the cute little gray box that Steve Jobs designed, had one serious flaw: it wasn't *expandable*. Other than a printer and a floppy disk drive, you couldn't plug anything into it. In fact, if you cracked open the case and looked inside, your warranty was voided!

The original IBM PCs, on the other hand, were designed with **expansion slots.** If you opened the computer's case, there were six slots, or open places, where optional circuit boards could be plugged in. This spawned an entire industry of add-on products, things like networking cards, internal modems, and tons of other goodies. This made the machine customizable and a lot more attractive to the buyer.

Apple quickly got the idea and changed their ways. They came out with the Mac II. It was designed to be opened up, and it also had six plug-ins, or slots, for expansion boards. The Mac couldn't use the same boards designed for the IBM PC because the Mac used a different type of connection called **NuBus.** NuBus was invented by Texas Instruments, and was considered a faster, smarter, superior type of slot. Soon all kinds of companies came out with boards for the Mac, (most of them video boards , 24-bit color boards for graphic designers and artists).

Apple soon did a weird thing—they started making many Macs with a different type of slot called **PDS** (Processor Direct Slot). NuBus cards didn't work in these types of slots unless you bought a $100 adapter from Apple, so this made adding cards pretty expensive.

Today, you can buy Macs with both type of slots and a new third kind called **PCI** (Peripheral Component Interconnect). PCI slots are compatible with those in the latest Intel/IBM-compatible computers, and they are very fast—cards plugged into these can communicate at two to three times the speed of NuBus. All the newest and most powerful Macintoshes have PCI.

If you own any Mac other than a Plus or earlier model, it's safe to say you have at least one of these slots built into your machine. Whether it's available or not is another issue. For example, if you have one of Apple's "DOS-compatible" Macintoshes, it probably had only one available slot and that's taken up with the DOS card.

Similarly, owners of the Power Mac 6100AV have their one available slot taken up by the AV card, making it impossible to plug in any other option.

PowerBook Expansion Slots

Recent PowerBooks (non-Duo models) can expand their hardware through **PC** cards.

The PC card slot design came from the world of the IBM-compatible notebook computers and had become a standard for almost all portable computers, including handheld ones like the Newton. Usually PC cards come in the form of modems and removable storage cards.

The SCSI Port

Some people complain that the Mac is not as expandable as other computers because they don't have as many expansion slots. Hooey.

Since 1986, every Mac has had a **SCSI** (Small Computer Systems Interface) connection on the back. This is a high speed data transfer connection that allows you to daisychain up to six external devices. That means you can plug an external CD-ROM drive into the back of the computer, and then plug a scanner into that, and they both work. In theory you can add a maximum of six devices, and they all work.

I say "in theory" because after three or so different devices are plugged in, things often get flaky—some devices may not be recognized, the Mac may not start up, and other weirdness may happen. People refer to this type of thing as "SCSI voodoo."

Luckily, if you know some of the methods used by the gurus to keep things going, you'll rarely have problems:

- **Make sure each device has a different ID number assigned to it.**
  Almost all external SCSI devices have a way to assign the SCSI ID number. Just look around on the case for two little black buttons with a number in the middle. Click the

buttons to change the number. Don't use 0 (zero) because zero is the ID number assigned to the internal hard disk on almost all Macs.

SCSI devices usually have a switch that looks something like this (but much tinier). This is where you change the ID number.

■ Use good, thick cables.

El Cheapo SCSI cables can cause tons of problems. In general, a thick cable is more reliable than a thin one. Apple is known for the quality (and high prices) of their cables. If you're having problems, try a different cable and see what happens.

■ Terminate!

You've probably seen those strange little plastic things with two wire hooks coming off the sides. They look kind of like the end of a SCSI cable, but without the cable attached. These little goodies are called **terminators,** and they are designed to be plugged into the last item (generally) of the SCSI chain. The purpose of the terminator is to tell the data flowing through the cables that this is the end of the line—now turn around and go back. Without a terminator, the data virtually falls off a cliff and you have problems. Plug the terminator into the open SCSI connection on the last device in the chain, and you should have smooth sailing. Some devices are terminated internally.

Termination is truly voodoo. If one arrangement of your daisy chain doesn't work, try connecting the devices in a different order, connecting the cables differently (the top port this time, instead of the bottom port, for instance) and, again, terminating the last device in the chain. Once you get an arrangement to work, leave it alone. If you ever have to take the setup apart, write down the order of devices that worked. Write down whether you plugged the cable into the top port or the bottom port. Write down whether you had to turn on the different devices in a certain order. And cross your fingers.

Acceleration and Upgrades

Upgrades

Apple and other manufacturers can perform surgery on your current Mac to bring it up the level of a newer, faster machine. People ask me all the time about whether this is the way to go, as generally these upgrades seem reasonably priced. Most of the time it's a bad idea. Here's why:

Look in the back and in the want ads of *Macworld* or *MacUser* magazine to see what your used computer is selling for. Then price a new system that is the equivalent of what you want to upgrade to. Calculate the difference, and compare that to the upgrade fee. Almost always you'd end up spending more money for the upgrade.

Acceleration is an even worse deal, generally. I can speed up my IIci to the equivalent speed of a 68040 Mac with an accelerator board, but I still have the old ROMs. What can happen is that an accelerated Mac will get confused—the ROM chips think the processor is different from the one actually installed. This incompatibility will cause some programs to freak out. I've never heard of someone buying an accelerator without having at least one of their programs "break."

The only times I suggest upgrading is when:

- The old machine has a bunch of expensive RAM
  in it that can't be used in a newer machine,
  or can't be sold for a decent price.

- The accelerator is a IIci cache card—
  very cheap, fast, and super-compatible.

- Sentimental Value: I must admit that I have, indeed,
  accelerated older computers myself, but those were CPUs
  near and dear to my heart—my first Mac for example.

Important Things to Remember

- Every Mac model has slightly different ROM chips, and the ROM chips act as part of the computer's central nervous system.

- Macintoshes are either Power Macs (using the PowerPC chip) or regular Macs using a 68040, 030, 020, or 68000 processor.

- To upgrade your RAM, you may have to remove existing RAM chips.

- On many Macs you can upgrade your VRAM to show more colors on-screen.

- Use good cables and terminators on SCSI devices.

- Don't upgrade your Mac—you deserve a new one.

Master Your System Folder 2

Your System Folder Has Too Much Stuff in It!

What if I told you there was a free way to:

- Make your Mac start up significantly faster.
- Seriously reduce crashes, freezes, and lockups.
- Free up several hundred kilobytes or even megabytes of usable RAM.

How is this possible? Easy—**clean out your System Folder!** Even if you have never added or installed anything on your computer, your System Folder is probably bloated with totally unnecessary software that can be removed (or preferably disabled) with no ill effects.

How did this happen? Simple. Apple set up a System Folder for you that would be sure to work with almost any configuration of printers, networks, modems, and application programs. In addition, they plugged in features they thought were neat. Often these are things that no one (almost) uses in real life. Removing (or at least disabling) these System add-ons will give you the three benefits listed above.

An example? I had a client who bought a new Performa a few months ago; it booted fine, but would lock up after an hour or so of playing Lode Runner (a program that came pre-loaded on the machine). First, we restarted the machine and held down the Shift key, making all Extensions and Control Panels inactive. This solved the crashing problem, but turned off many important features—like being able to use the CD-ROM drive. Since we now knew one or more of these programs in the System Folder was the culprit, we launched the **Extensions Manager** program, disabled a few of the superfluous Extensions and Control Panels Apple installed in the System Folder, and soon we were bulletproof (crash-free).

Why do these add-ons cause problems? That's a tougher question to answer. One thing to keep in mind is that *all programs are defective.* The old adage "never buy a program with a .0 on the end" bears some discussion. The first release of some programs (Word 3.0, System 6.0) had catastrophic bugs. Almost every other program I know of with a .0 on the end has been quickly upgraded to 3.01 or 6.01 as the initial flaws were discovered and corrected. This process never ends. As more problems are found and corrected others crop up. The software you buy is never completely purged of the bugs that exist.

Another important concept is that programs *fight with each other.* Every program you run—System, Finder, Extensions, Control Panels, and applications—uses various parts of your computer's hardware to make things happen. Sometimes two programs ask for the same thing at the same time (Extensions and Control Panels are notorious for this). For example, as of this writing, if you have Apple Menu Options 1.1.2 active in your System Folder and try certain operations in Word 6.0, you'll be in crash city. I have no idea why they're incompatible, but they are. Although this is an extreme example, all Extensions and Control Panels have the potential to cause conflicts.

Also, you need to remember that programs and files can become **corrupted.** Due to a variety of reasons, software that worked great one day can become damaged the next and cause constant crashes and lockups.

You combine these three facts and it becomes clear: Run your Mac as lean and mean as possible!

What's Really Important?

Life used to be so easy for us Mac users. My first System Folder had three main files in it: System, Finder, and the ImageWriter printer driver. It was clear what did what and how to control the situation. Best of all, it took up only 300K of disk space.

Today, my System Folder is 42 megabytes, has 1,000 items in it, and many items have names and icons that you need a Ph.D. to understand—intuitive names like "A/ROSE" and "InputBackSupport."

The problem is, to be a true power user you have to know what most of these items do, how they should be organized, what problems they can cause, and most importantly—*which ones to get rid of!* That's the point of this chapter—identifying files and organizing your System Folder so you get maximum performance and minimum hassles.

Your Mac only needs three items in the System Folder to operate in a basic fashion: the System file, the Finder, and an Enabler file (an Enabler may not be a requirement on your Macintosh). If you throw everything else away (don't!), you'll still be able to reboot the machine. (True, your Mac will recreate the Fonts, Extensions, Apple Menu Items, Control Panels, and Preferences *folders,* but they'll be empty.)

The **System file** is the real workhorse here. It contains the "smarts" of the operating system. Not surprisingly, it is also the largest of the three. It is powerful enough that some Macs in rare instances can run in a limited fashion with only the System file present.

The **Finder's** job is to present you with a pretty face for control over filing things. Folders, icons, and the Trash are controlled by the Finder. Apple originally called it the "Filer," but legal hurdles (someone else owned the name) forced a last-minute name change to Finder. This is why being "in the Finder" or "switching to the Finder" means going to where you do filing.

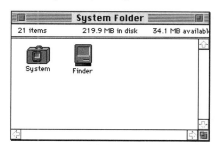

Your Mac could probably operate with just these items in the System Folder . . .

. . . although after restart, it would rebuild some necessary items.

Enablers were introduced a few years back because Apple got tired of issuing a new System and Finder every time they brought out a new Macintosh model. Remember from our discussion about hardware (Chapter One) that part of a Mac's personality comes from its ROM chip. Every Mac model has slightly different ROM instructions built into it, so in the old days (before 1989) Apple would bring out a new Mac and the new ROMs would have additional capabilities that the existing System and Finder couldn't take advantage of. Apple's solution was to issue totally new System software with most new Macs—software that you could install on older Macs as well.

Here's the most dramatic example—when Apple came out with the Mac II, it had very different ROMs with many new capabilities. Unlike all Macs built previously, this new Mac could do color, accept expansion cards, and was able to handle more than 4 megabytes of RAM. The existing System software (version 3.2) could not run on this new machine, as it was designed for Macs with none of those capabilities—you had to run the new version 4.1.

Today when Apple ships a new machine it just creates a new Enabler for it. Use the existing System software, drop the new Enabler in, and it will "tweak" the System and Finder every time you restart so they know how to work with this new machine.

Other than the System, Finder, and maybe an Enabler, everything else in your System Folder is optional. Keeping this in mind, it's clear that you can probably disengage many of the several hundred other items in there and still have a workable configuration.

The first thing to memorize is this: **Don't add things** to your System Folder unless you absolutely, for-sure, no-other-choice, have to. If your Mac is running okay, **leave it alone!** Several times a month clients call and say something like, "Steve! My Mac is suddenly crashing all the time!" Ninety percent of them have just installed the latest greatest version of MacCool Utilities or some other piece of software that puts twelve new Extensions and Control Panels in their System Folder. Invariably I ask, "Okay, so what does this new program do for you that is so important?" Rarely is there a real need for this new program, so I tell them to get rid of it. That can be hard to do, as you don't always know what's been added. One easy way to protect yourself is to always keep a clean (and very recent) backup of your System Folder so you can just replace the one that's screwed up. On page 67 I describe a technique for finding out exactly what this new program added to your System Folder without your permission.

Extensions and Control Panel Management Programs

Pruning your System Folder used to mean clawing through the various folders and files and manually dragging the unwanted items out — either into an outside folder or directly into the trash.

A much easier (not to mean safer) way exists today: **extension managers.** Extension managers are programs that allow you to turn Control Panels and Extensions off and on without having to drag anything around. It's a simple matter of checking off the ones you don't want (disabled files automatically get moved to special folders where they're not noticed the next time you startup). One of the best things about these managers is that they can create different "startup sets" you can use in different situations.

There are a half-dozen good extension managers available. I'll describe the one most people use. It comes free with the Mac, and surprisingly it's called **Extensions Manager.**

To bring it up, choose the **Control Panels** item under the Apple Menu, and then choose the **Extensions Manager.**

Once this is up, you'll see a scrolling list of items that you can make active or inactive: click a checkmark next to the item on or off. The tough part is determining which ones to keep active and which ones to disengage. Let's go through all the Apple Extensions and Control Panels in a logical fashion.

Apple's original Extensions Manager (below) is very simple to understand. You just click a checkmark next to the items you want "on."

Apple's latest and greatest Extensions Manager comes with System 7.6. Like the old Extensions Manager, it lets you put checkmarks next to Extensions and Control Panels you want on.

Besides displaying more Extensions and Control Panels than the old manager, this new one can also group Extensions by function.

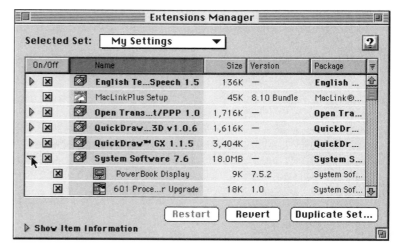

First, we'll go through the all-important Extensions and Control Panels that everyone should leave activated. Then we'll look at the ones almost nobody should use—ones that I feel practically everybody can turn off without ill effects.

Then we'll start to look at what kind of hardware and peripherals you work with, as well as what kind of work you do. This will allow us to turn off the rest of these unneeded programs. We'll generally go from least common scenarios to most common.

Don't worry if I describe a Control Panel or Extension that you don't see listed in your Extensions Manager. Not all Macs will have all these. Just turn on or off the ones that are listed.

Keepers: Crucial Extensions and Control Panels

Keep and learn to use the following files in your System Folder.

Date & Time

The **Date & Time** Control Panel does just what it says— it's for setting the date and time. Also use it for configuring the appearance of the clock that appears on the menu bar.

Find File Extension

The **Find File** extension enhances the standard Find File command with additional criteria for searching and lists found items in the Find File window.

Monitors & Sound

Monitors & Sound is used to configure color and resolution of your monitor as well as the volumes of your speakers and microphones. On some Macs, you may just find the **Sound** Control Panel. Keep it active.

Mouse

Mouse is nice to have around, although it's not life-threatening to remove it. This Control Panel lets you control how fast your mouse works.

Memory

The **Memory** Control Panel is absolutely essential. Programs use memory in different ways, and this utility lets you make changes as needed. See Chapter Three for more information.

General Controls

It's a good idea to always have these items available.

Use the **General Controls** Control Panel to control cursor actions, where new documents should be stored, System Folder protection, application switching, and a few other details.

AppleScript

With AppleScript you can write mini-programs that will automate procedures in your existing Mac programs. Unfortunately, very few real-world users actually write and use scripts because script writing isn't easy and not many programs are scriptable.

Nevertheless, I tell people to leave this turned on. Many programs these days assume it's present, and may not function correctly if it has been turned off. Keep the following active:

AppleScript

AppleScript Lib

Finder Scripting Extension

InLineFilter

Clipping Extension

The Clipping Extension makes it possible to drag-and-drop text and graphics onto the Desktop.

Startup Disk Control Panel

The Startup Disk Control Panel lets you set which disk should take charge on startup. It is vital for some troubleshooting operations.

Keepers: Harmless Items

You probably don't need most of these items, but they don't get activated at startup like other Extensions or Control Panels anyway. These are mostly items that other programs may refer to for information. They generally don't take up RAM, and have little to no chance of causing conflicts.

A good rule of thumb is if it has the words Shared, Library, Lib, or Tool in the name, you can leave it alone. Some of these include:

Apple Modem Tool
ObjectSupportLib
OpenTpt AppleTalk Library
OpenTpt Internet Library
OpenTransport Library
OpenTptAppleTalkLib
OpenTptInternetLib
OpenTransportLib
PrintingLib
Serial Tool
Shared Library Manager
Shared Library Manager PPC
Text Tool
TTY Tool
XMODEM Tool

Other harmless items include:

OpenTpt Modem
OpenTpt Modem 68K
OpenTpt Remote Access
OpenTpt Remote Access 68K
OpenTpt Serial Arbitrator
Serial (Built-in)

Bloatware: Terminate with Prejudice

Here are the programs that are either: a) worthless, b) cause more problems than they solve, or c) needed by so few people that you should feel confident in the safety of turning them off.

Screen Savers

Forget everything people have told you about how your screen can be affected by "burn in." You know what I mean—if you leave the same image showing on your screen for a long time, it eventually damages the phosphor and leaves a permanent impression. This is the theory behind programs like **After Dark** and **UnderWare**—software that after five or ten minutes of no mouse or keyboard activity causes a random moving pattern to take over the screen.

Be afraid.
Be very afraid.

Color monitors are practically immune to this, and PowerBook screens are *impossible* to burn in. Even if they weren't, or if you are one of the sixteen people (like me) in North America still using a black-and-white screen, there's this cute little item on our monitor called a dimmer switch! We can use this amazing feature should we go on vacation and want to leave our computer turned on.

I learned the hard way the perils of screen savers. My first experience was a few years ago when I kept crashing during long print jobs. It seemed that when the flying toasters kicked in, they'd get into a turf battle with my printing software and the whole system would freak out.

Recently a coworker violated our office-wide "no screen saver" policy and insisted on installing a nifty program that would bring up random art masterpieces from the Louvre. Suddenly, the entire tape backup system for the office stopped working. After days of playing with the network, we discovered a conflict between the two programs.

Turn off After Dark, UnderWare, or anything with "screen saver" in the name.

WorldScript

Starting with System 7.1, Apple has had available a set of international language Extensions. If you need to switch between typing English and Kanji for example, the WorldScript Extensions make this easy. Since you probably don't need this capability, nuke the following:

WorldScript Power Adapter

WorldScript I

WorldScript II

InputBackSupport

Text

QuickTime Musical Instruments

Apple has ingeniously incorporated a MIDI sound system into their QuickTime Multimedia software, which allows software developers to create tiny sound files that sound like an orchestra when played back with this Extension. It's amazing, it's wonderful, but since few developers have created any uses for it, you can turn it off for now.

PowerTalk

System 7.5 came with an interesting set of software utilities from Apple called PowerTalk, which gave you a uniform way to receive and send messages with your computer. It included a simple electronic mail system, and even had ways for applications to talk to each other. The problem? It's a RAM hog and hardly anyone uses it. Odds are you don't either. Even Apple finally gave up and discontinued it. Disable the following:

PowerTalk Extension

PowerTalk Manager

PowerTalk Setup

Macintosh Easy Open (also called Mac OS Easy Open)

Let's say someone gives you a document they created in WordPerfect, and you don't have WordPerfect installed on your computer. If you double-click the document, it tells your Mac to launch WordPerfect and open the file. Since you don't have that application, you'll probably get an "Application busy or missing" error message.

Macintosh Easy Open is a neat program designed to fix this. You can tell Easy Open that WordPerfect files should be automatically opened in Word, or that Lotus 1-2-3 files should launch in Excel if you double-click them. (Naturally, you can't do something like tell Excel to open a scanned photo—they're just too different.)

My advice is to disable Macintosh Easy Open anyway. It may slow down some operations, can cause spontaneous desktop rebuilding on startup, and can have significant conflicts with other programs. Besides, you can open those files another easy way—just drag the document icon onto the program you want it to open with, as shown below.

text file

Microsoft Excel alias

Press on the document icon and drag it to the icon or alias of the program you want to open it in.

text file

Microsoft Excel alias

If that application can open the document, its icon will highlight. Just let go of the document—it will launch the app and open the file.

QuickDraw GX

Another interesting idea. QuickDraw GX is a printing architecture introduced by Apple a few years ago that permits fonts to have many more characters, foreign character sets, drag-and-drop printer icons (the ability to drag a document to a printer icon and have it print), and more power over advanced typographic features like ligatures.

The problem is that very few (almost zero) software vendors have written programs that support GX, and it takes up a hefty amount of RAM. Deactivate:

QuickDraw GX

QuickDraw GX Helper

ATM GX

PrinterShare GX

3-Hole Punch

Letterhead

N–Up Printing

Stationery

QuickDraw 3D

I feel terrible putting QuickDraw 3D under this category, as it's a great Extension that lets you create and view 3D worlds. There are some neat sites on the Internet that let you take advantage of this software, but not enough to make it a keeper. Turn off the following:

QuickDraw™ 3D

QuickDraw™ 3D RAVE

QuickDraw™ 3D Viewer

Unneeded Printer Drivers

Disable all of the printer drivers that don't apply to you (meaning you don't have that kind of printer connected to your Mac):

AppleTalk ImageWriter, Color SW 2200, Color SW 2400, Color SW 2500, Color SW Pro, ImageWriter, LaserWriter, Laser-Writer 300, LaserWriter 8, LaserWriter 8f, LW Select 310, Personal LaserWriter SC, StyleWriter 1200, StyleWriter II Color SW 1500

IR Talk

Many PowerBooks have an infrared transmission port. Using this software, they can connect with an AppleTalk network without cables. It requires special infrared receiving hardware attached to your network at the office. You may be the one-in-a-million using it, but I'm betting you can kill IR Talk.

A/ROSE

A/ROSE is required for some obscure network interface cards such as the Apple Token Ring 4.16 NB card and the Apple Serial NB card (both discontinued long ago) to function properly. Millions of people have this thing installed and don't need it.

Cache Switch

If you have a 68040 Mac, turning off the Cache Switch can prevent some ancient software programs from crashing. It does nothing for Power Macs or non-68040 machines.

Serial Switch

The Mac IIfx and the Quadra 950 have a special serial port that works in conjunction with this Control Panel. You can use the Serial Switch to set the port on those machines to work at a special faster speed. The problem is that a lot of programs freak out if you do this.

Button Disabler

The Button Disabler disables the volume and brightness controls on the front of Mac or Performa 500 series computers. The idea was to keep kids from messing with the controls. Even if you have small children, you'll probably never use it.

Color

The Color Control Panel lets you change the highlight color and window color scheme. You can go years without ever touching it, so you might as well disable it.

You Probably Don't Need . . .

If you've deactivated the items I've discussed so far, you've gained a lot of speed, reliability, and memory. Here are more things most people can turn off. Leave these items on only if they apply to you.

Professional Color Management

ColorSync is a set of Extensions and Control Panels that help graphic professionals maintain color accuracy between scanning, viewing, and printing. Even many graphic experts don't utilize this software. Disable:

> ColorSync
> ColorSync System Profile

To Access Your Office Network from Home

Apple Remote Access is a very, very, neat set of software that lets you connect to the office network remotely (with a modem). The idea is that you can be far away from the office and still access servers and disks in the office, send internal e-mail, and even print!

While many people take advantage of this great capability, most do not. If you don't, you can disengage:

> Apple Remote Access Client
> Link Tool Manager
> Modem Link Tool Personal
> Remote Only
> Serial Port Arbitrator
> DialAssist
> Remote Access Setup

Unsupported Online Help

Although it's a critically acclaimed online help system, **Apple Guide** is not well supported, and it takes up quite a bit of RAM (40K or so). As a new Mac user, you probably kept it on and maybe even used it a few times to learn the basics.

Most users never touch it, and since I assume you're beyond the basic level—turn it off.

A Talking Mac

Speech Manager can read text files in a humanlike voice. I think I'm one of the few people on the planet who actually gets some use out of it—I describe in Chapter Eleven a great use for a talking Mac. Despite my enthusiasm, most people will want it off.

> Speech Manager
> Speech

Cute Little Gadgets that Don't Do Much

These are a few items that are admittedly useful, but you might want to weigh their usefulness with their innate ability to cause conflict.

The **Energy Saver Control Panel** and the **Energy Saver Extension** work together. They allow you to put some Macs to sleep, either after a certain period of inactivity or at a specified time. They can also restart a Mac at a pre-selected time—for midnight downloads and the like. I say get rid of them—particularly if you have an AppleVison 1710 monitor as they can damage the display. I prefer to just turn off the monitor using its power switch.

WindowShade is a nifty little program that began its life as shareware. Install it, and you can collapse palettes and windows down to just their title bar by double-clicking on the bar. I use Adobe Illustrator a lot, and WindowShade is great for manipulating the palettes. For most users though, it's not worth it.

Apple Menu Options adds hierarchical submenus to the Apple Menu; that is, it lists items in a menu rather than opening the folders themselves. It also serves as a cheap alternative to Super Boomerang (from Now Utilities, see page 132), as it remembers recently opened applications and files. I leave it off and use Boomerang instead.

A neat program you should probably turn off.

Auto Power On/Off is a program that allows you to set a time for your Mac to automatically shut itself down. It doesn't work with all Macs.

Launcher creates a floating palette with buttons that represent files and programs, which makes launching applications and documents easier. Most gurus shy away from it. Aliases on the desktop seem to work just as well for most people. I use QuicKeys to launch applications and Super Boomerang to open files—see Chapter Seven for more info.

Desktop Patterns allows you to change your background pattern on your Desktop.

Color lets you set the highlight color that will appear when you select something, as well as the border color of your windows.

The **Keyboard** Control Panel lets you set the key repeat rate and other settings. Odds are you've never touched it.

It's the same thing with **Labels.** While I use it quite a bit to customize my Labels menu, you probably don't have any plans for it.

You may have played with the **Map.** It lets you check time zones and distances between cities. Its list of cities is quite incomplete, so it is of little real value. Do look for "Nowhere" on the map, though.

The **Numbers** Control Panel is another set-and-forget item. It lets you define how numbers are displayed on your Mac. You can tell it where to put commas, dollar signs, etc.

The **Views** Control Panel allows you to modify how the items in the windows are displayed. If you use it and like it, keep it.

Crash-Prone Printing Enhancements

These are controversial choices on my part. The following all make printing more convenient and easier—however, they do not add any new capabilities to your printer. Many of my associates totally disagree with my choice to turn all of these programs off (my associates also crash a lot more than I do). Try working with and without the following items.

PrintMonitor

PrintMonitor is a program designed to trick your Mac into thinking it's finished printing something before it actually has. The idea is this: you hit the Print command, PrintMonitor wakes up and starts intercepting the data and immediately "spools" it off to your hard disk. The program you're printing from thinks the printer has taken all the data and has printed your page. The spooled data is then dribbled off to the printer in the background.

The good news is that you don't have to wait for something to print before you can go back to work on the computer. The bad news is that it actually takes longer to print, and you **will** crash more.

Desktop Printer Extension

Desktop Printer Extension works in conjunction with version 8.3 and above printer drivers. It allows you to create icons on your desktop that represent the printers you're connected to. This permits drag-and-drop printing. Handy, but it's another item that may cause conflicts.

Desktop Printer Spooler, Desktop PrintMonitor, and Desktop Printer Menu

Desktop Printer Spooler and PrintMonitor work in conjunction with the LaserWriter 8.3 driver and above and the Desktop Printer Extension to allow spooling and scheduling of print jobs sent to printers through their desktop icons. Desktop Printer Menu adds a new menu that makes it easier to choose a printer. Once again—you get a bunch of neat features and more crashes.

Printer Share

If you have an inkjet printer, it's probably set up so that just one Mac can print to it—the Mac it's attached to. If you activate PrinterShare on the computer attached to the printer, other Macs on the network can also use this printer.

To Access DOS or Windows Disks

Don't get me wrong—I know there are millions of Mac users who need access to PC disks. It's just that most do it rarely or never. I advise you to leave the following off and activate them when you need to access DOS/Windows files.

PC Exchange

untitled

Mount PC disks on your Mac with PC Exchange.

Every Macintosh built since 1987 has a disk drive that is physically capable of using PC/DOS/Windows disks (the only exception is the Mac Plus—discontinued in 1990). The reality is that you also need special software to make a PC disk work like a Mac disk, otherwise your computer will try and reformat the PC disk.

PC Exchange is that software. If you leave this on, you can "transparently" use PC disks (make them act like Mac disks).

MacLinkPlus Setup

MacLinkPlus converts DOS and Windows documents into Mac equivalents. For example, if someone gives you a Lotus 1-2-3 file on a floppy disk, MacLinkPlus can automatically convert it to an Excel spreadsheet when you copy that file to your hard drive.

This differs from Macintosh Easy Open, which doesn't actually convert anything. MacLinkPlus transforms a 1-2-3 file into an Excel file when you copy it onto your hard disk; Easy Open asks Excel to convert and open the file.

You Need to Decide . . .

Leave these Extensions and Control Panels off unless the following apply to you.

Are You Physically Challenged?

Close View

CloseView is a Control Panel that enables you to greatly magnify portions of your screen. It is invaluable for those who need help seeing small type and graphics.

Easy Access

Easy Access permits the keyboard to serve as a replacement for the mouse.

Do You Have a:

Mac Classic?

Keep the Brightness Control Panel active. It lets you adjust your monitor's brightness and contrast.

Power Mac 7200?

The Power Mac 7200 has a graphics accelerator chip. The **7200 Graphics Acceleration Extension** allows that particular computer (only) to take advantage of this additional processor. Without it, the CPU chip takes the load, slowing things down a bit.

5200, 5300 or 6200 series Mac?

The **Processor Info Extension** fixes a minor speed-reporting bug on those machines only.

Power Mac 6100AV, 7100AV, 8100AV?

You'll want to keep the **PowerPC Monitors Extension.** It allows for proper video-out on those models.

Monitor with no control knobs?

If you have a Mac with the monitor attached directly to the CPU and no manual contrast/brightness controls, the **Screen Control Panel** is the only way to change those settings. This program can also automatically dim the screen after a defined period of inactivity.

ATI Video Card?

You may want to leave the Graphics Accelerator Extension active because it can make video operations on your Mac faster. There have been some incompatibilities and crashes with it in the past.

An Apple AV Monitor?

The 14AV, 15AV, and 17AV need the **PowerPC Monitors Extension.**

Apple Video Player?

The **Video Startup Extension** is required for the player to work.

Do You Have Little Kids?

At Ease restricts user access to the Finder. It is used mostly to keep children from moving files around and throwing things in the Trash. If this doesn't sound like you, disable **At Ease 7.5 Startup** and **At Ease 7.5 Layer Patch.**

Do You Access the Internet?

You should read Chapter 12 about getting on the Web to better understand what these items can do for you.

TCP/IP

TCP/IP is networking software required by many Internet providers to connect to their system.

Config PPP

Config PPP is software used to call and make a connection to your provider.

MacTCP

MacTCP is most often used to permit Internet access, but can also be used for local area networks (networks within your building).

Modem Control Panel

The Modem Control Panel works with Apple's Open Transport to let you change your modem settings.

PPP Control Panel

The PPP Control Panel works with Apple's Open Transport to allow your Mac to use the Internet's point-to-point protocol.

Do You Have a PowerBook?

If not, you can disable everything listed below. If you are a Power-Book user, I'll describe what these things do so you can check off the ones you don't need:

Control Strip

Originally just a PowerBook thing (now available on all Macs), the **Control Strip** Control Panel creates an easily accessed bar on your screen that contains buttons for quickly customizing your Mac's operation.

The buttons that appear on the Control Strip are installed in the **Control Strip Modules folder** inside your System Folder. I use the Control Strip all the time on my PowerBook, but not as often on my desktop machine.

The Control Strip is really handy on PowerBooks and now can also be used on all Macs.

Assistant Toolbox

This Extension performs a myriad of useful (albeit obscure) tasks. Assistant Toolbox helps perform file synchronization, enables keyboard shortcuts for sleep and hard disk spindown, and has other goodies such as deferred printing and e-mail sending. It also allows your PowerBook to remember the contents of a RAM disk when you restart.

Caps Lock

Caps Lock creates an on-screen indicator in the Menu bar to let you know when you have the Caps Lock key depressed.

PC Card Extension

Use PC Card Extension on newer PowerBooks that use special PC cards. This Extension must be activated for the card to be recognized.

AutoRemounter

If you have a PowerBook and access someone else's hard disk over a network, putting your Mac to sleep causes your computer to "forget" about that other hard disk, and it disappears from your Desktop. AutoRemounter will force the accessed disk to magically reappear when you wake up the Mac.

PowerBook

The PowerBook Control Panel lets you specify how a Power-Book uses and conserves power. I'd leave it on.

PC Card Modem Extension

Newer PowerBooks that have PC modem cards installed need the PC Card Modem Extension for the modem to be recognized.

PowerBook Setup

If you use your PowerBook as an external SCSI hard disk, PowerBook Setup lets you change SCSI ID numbers. It also permits you to set a time for a wake-up call that brings your PowerBook out of sleep mode unattended. Neither of these are very important for most users.

If you disable this, you will still be able to SCSI dock your PowerBook to another computer; you just won't be able to alter the ID number.

PowerBook Monitors Extension

If you plug external monitors into your PowerBook, this Extension provides some control over how they operate.

PowerBook Display

If you want to hook your PowerBook into an external projector to make a presentation, this Control Panel provides you with options to make the connection easier.

Password Security

You can prevent unauthorized people from waking or starting up your PowerBook by creating a password with this Control Panel.

Power Macintosh Card

Even if you have a PowerBook, you probably don't have one that was upgraded to a PowerPC chip. This Extension is required for people who had their 68040 PowerBook accelerated.

Trackpad

PowerBooks with built-in trackpads use this Control Panel to affect responsiveness.

Do You Need to Network/Share Files?

If you don't have your computer connected to anyone else's computer, you can eliminate these items.

AppleShare

AppleShare is a Chooser item required for you to access other people's hard disks ("remote volumes" in geekspeak).

File Sharing Extension

The File Sharing Extension allows you to share your hard disk(s) or folders with others.

Network Extension

The Network Extension works in conjunction with the Network or AppleTalk Control Panels. It allows you to access a network and to turn on File Sharing.

Network Control Panel

On older, non-Open Transport configured Macintoshes, the Network Control Panel lets you choose what type of network to connect to.

AppleTalk

The AppleTalk Control Panel is used with the Open Transport networking software to configure an AppleTalk connection.

File Sharing Monitor Control Panel

If you have File Sharing turned on, the File Sharing Monitor lets you see who is accessing your hard disks and folders.

Sharing Setup Control Panel

Sharing Setup is the master Control Panel that lets you turn sharing on or off and establish your ownership password.

Users & Groups

When you have File Sharing turned on, the settings made in the Users & Groups Control Panel establishes who has access to which disks and folders.

Are You Connected to an Ethernet Network?

If you are not networking at all, or are using LocalTalk as your method for connecting computers, you can disconnect all of these:

Apple Ethernet CS II

Ethernet (Built-In)

EtherTalk Phase 2

Apple Built-In Ethernet

Apple Ethernet CS

Apple Ethernet LC

Apple Ethernet NB

Are You Connected to a Token Ring Network?

If not, disengage the following:

Apple PCI Token Ring

TokenTalk Phase 2

TokenTalk Prep

Apple Token Ring NB

Token Ring

Do You Have to Use Microsoft Applications?

Microsoft OLE Extension

Object Linking and Embedding (OLE) is Microsoft's approach to integrating live data between applications. The Microsoft OLE Extension permits you to do things like put an Excel spreadsheet inside a report you've done in Word. If you run Word, Excel, or PowerPoint you'll want this (even if you don't want to integrate those files). Otherwise, it grabs a lot of resources; disable it.

Shared Code Manager

Shared Code Manager lets Microsoft applications share the same software code among several programs. Keep it if you run several Microsoft apps.

Microsoft Office Manager

Microsoft Office Manager puts a new menu listing available Microsoft applications at the top of your screen. It makes it easier to launch those apps, but is not worth the lockups and crashes. Nuke it.

Do You Run Multimedia Programs?

QuickTime

Almost all interactive CDs require the QuickTime Extension to be active. It permits standard animations, movies, and sound files to run. Graphics professionals also need this Extension to perform some types of image compression.

QuickTime PowerPlug

QuickTime PowerPlug is a PowerPC Patch for QuickTime. It allows Power Macs to run QuickTime efficiently.

Audio Volume Extension

If you have a 5200, 5300, 6200, or 6300 series Mac and an internal modem, the Audio Volume Extension software helps control the sounds it emits. It also controls some sounds played from CD-ROMs.

QuickTime Settings

The QuickTime Settings Control Panel lets you make adjustments to audio CDs and allows you to configure how QuickTime Musical Instruments play.

QuickTime Musical Instruments

As mentioned previously, even if you are running multimedia programs you should turn this off.

Do You Have a CD-ROM Drive?

If so, keep some or all of the following active. If not, turn off:

Apple CD-ROM

A must-have for using an Apple CD-ROM drive. Apple CD-ROM is the driver that allows your computer to sense the presence of the drive.

Foreign File Access

When used in conjunction with a standard CD-ROM driver such as Apple CD-ROM, Foreign File Access allows the drive to access photo-CD formatted disks. If you're using primarily multimedia CDs, turn it off until you need it.

AppleCD Audio Player

AppleCD Audio Player lets you play music CDs in the drive.

Now Toolbox Info

Now Toolbox
A component of Now Utilities™ 5.0
Kind: system extension
Size: 90K on disk (91,439 bytes used)
Where: APS Drive™: System Folder :
Extensions :
Created: Tue, Apr 21, 1992, 9:38 AM
Modified: Mon, May 20, 1996, 7:31 PM
Version: 5.0.0B, ©1992-94 Now Software,
Inc.
Comments:

☐ **Locked**

The Get Info box can clue you in on what company produced the Extension and maybe even what it does.

Non-Apple Extensions

You have no doubt discovered a dozen or two Extensions and/or Control Panels installed on your machine that we haven't discussed. These are probably files installed for other non-Apple programs to take advantage of. My advice is to look through your software manual indices for descriptions of what they do and determine the best action to take. I use Get Info to find out what company created the program— that usually gives me a clue which manual to look in.

- Click once on an icon, then press Command I,
  or choose "Get Info" from the File menu.

Sometimes, if I have trouble finding out what one of these does, I'll just turn it off and see what happens. If a program needs something you've disabled, you'll usually get an error message when you launch the application that will tell you to put it back.

Extensions that Refuse to Leave

Okay—so if you turn Extensions and Control Panels off, they get moved into special "disabled" folders. The problem is, some items don't get recognized by Extensions Manager and so they stay put— even if you tell the Manager to disable everything!

Control Panels (Disabled)

Extensions (Disabled)

Extensions Manager creates these folders and puts deactivated programs into them.

Many of these items are simply ignored when you start up again, because they need another Extension to activate them. A good example is "About Apple Guide"; this will stay in your Extensions folder even if you disengage Apple Guide itself.

My advice is: don't worry about them too much. At most they add only a couple hundred K to your RAM usage, and they may be important should you decide to reactivate some disabled component.

The only time I've had to get in there and wrestle with those ignored Extensions was when we had a problem machine that ran fine after a Shift key restart (a Shift-Restart causes everything in the Control Panels or Extensions folders to be totally ignored without actually moving them). We started turning off Extensions and Control Panels one by one, hoping to find the problem program. Soon we had *all* of them off, and we were still crashing! Turns out, we had a corrupted file in the Control Panels folder that wasn't recognized by the Extensions Manager so we had to remove it manually.

Staying Clean

Dealing with Obnoxious Application Programs

Installing new application programs will almost always throw some new "goodies" into your System Folder. Be vigilant! As soon as you've installed a new application, open your Extensions Manager and see if you can figure out what's been added. If you can't tell what's new, try the following trick described by Joseph Schorr in *Macworld* magazine. He described how to detect anything new installed in your System Folder and at the same time gave us a new use for Labels:

1. View your System Folder by Name.

2. Expand all folders in outline view (press Command A to select all, then press Command RightArrow).

3. Go to the Label Menu and choose a label.
   This will label everything in your System Folder. You might want to create a custom label like "Pre-Install" or something—just use the **Labels** Control Panel.

4. Install your new software.

5. Go back into the System Folder and see what does **not** have the special label.

   In the Finder, use the **Print Window** command under the **File Menu** to get a hard copy you can use later in case you need to "de-install" these files. Use a highlighter to mark the new files, and put the printout in the software box.

Hopefully, you can turn some of these components off and still run your software. Try it—disable anything new, restart, and see what happens. If the new component(s) are required, just use Extensions Manager to activate them again.

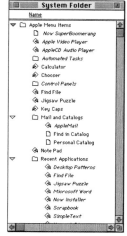

Command A plus Command RightArrow expands all subfolders in a window.

*(To **close** all expanded folders, press Command A to select them all, then press Command LeftArrow.)*

Then use labels to mark System Folder items prior to installing anything new.

Dealing with Well-Meaning Friends and CoWorkers

Often your brother-in-law will want to install some nifty new game or screen saver. He'll start tossing things into the System Folder, and soon this new gadget will be up and running. Things will seem okay for an hour or two, and then you'll try to print/quit/launch something. Up comes a system error dialog box, and it's restart time. Of course he's long gone, so you may not know what's been added or removed.

I never let anyone mess around with my System Folder. If you plan on giving someone this authority, make sure you get a complete list of what was put where.

The Secret to Using Tons of Extensions

Even though I run my machine with a very lean System, I can still take advantage of over 100 Control Panels and Extensions by specifying different **Startup Sets.** An example? I log onto the Internet maybe once a day. There are about a half-dozen Extensions I don't need for anything but Internet access. Rather than have all those running all the time, I have a special startup set just for when I'm online. This set has my Internet Extensions activated, and some of the other Extensions deactivated that I don't need when I'm online.

All I do is launch Extensions Manager, choose the Internet set, and restart. After I'm done online, I reinstate my "Standard" set and restart. True, it is a bit inconvenient to do multiple restarts, but the great thing is **I hardly ever crash.** Contrast this with my hotshot Mac coworkers who just leave everything on. They have to restart several times a day anyway (because they crash so often), and their restarts are agonizingly slow because crashed Macs need to rebuild system files that were damaged by the lockup. Another bonus is that a scheduled restart purges memory of fragmentation (see Chapter Three).

Create your own startup set

How do you create a custom startup set? Easy. Just bring up the Extensions Manager and choose which Extensions you want turned on/off. Next go to the **Sets** menu and save it, giving it a name.

Next time you want to switch sets, you can do one of two things:

- Bring up Extensions Manager, choose a set, and restart.
- Or restart, hold down the Spacebar, and the Manager will come up automatically, letting you choose a set. Just click the close box to continue the restart.

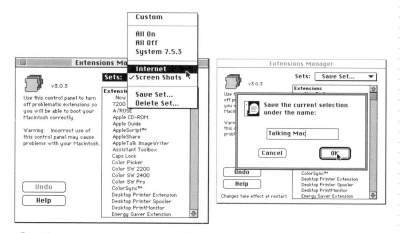

Creating your own startup sets is easy.

Closing Thoughts

There are other Extension Managers that have additional features. Now Utilities has **Now Startup Manager,** which does all the things that Apple's program does. It can also do things like change the order of when Extensions load (this can prevent some crashes) and run startup tests to find out which Extension or Control Panel is causing crashes. Some experts prefer **Conflict Catcher** by Casady and Greene, which does even more—I like how it can actually show you the names of the Extensions as they load, rather than just their cryptic icons. See Chapter Four, especially page 93, for more info.

My advice is get to know Apple's Extensions Manager before moving on to these others.

Important Things to Remember

- Don't add things to your System Folder unless you have no other choice.

- All Extensions and Control Panels have the potential to cause crashes and other problems.

- Minimize the number of Extensions and Control Panels that run on your System.

- The Extensions Manager is a great way to selectively turn Extensions and Control Panels on and off.

- Restart with the Shift key down to bypass all Extensions and Control Panels.

- Restart with the Spacebar down to bring up the Extensions Manager on startup.

- Make different customized sets of Extensions and Control Panels that can be activated under special circumstances.

Maximize Your Memory

3

Don't Let the Inmates Run the Asylum!

We all want our computers to be fast *and* bulletproof (crashing rarely). There are a few ways to achieve both goals at the same time. One is to minimize our Extensions and Control Panels (see Chapter Two). The other is to practice smart memory management.

It's easy to understand and control RAM usage on the Mac—in fact it's much easier than on any other platform. The problem is that almost no one does it! Letting your System, Finder, and software programs take charge of how much RAM they use is not only dangerous—it's downright expensive! Time is money—and you spend it recovering from crashes, waiting for sluggish programs to finish tasks, and trying to get around "not enough memory" messages.

Let's talk about a few simple things you can do to make a big difference in allocating your Mac's most precious resource—**memory.**

How Memory Gets Allocated

First let's look at how your Macintosh deals with memory.

System Heap

It all starts when you turn on your computer. When the System is turned off, the RAM chips are "empty." Nothing goes on inside them without power to keep refreshing the data. A few seconds after hitting the On switch, your operating System Software (the System, Finder, Extensions, and Control Panels) is activated and copied from the hard drive into RAM. (Okay, okay, I've oversimplified things—not *all* of this stuff gets copied, just the essential bits. For this discussion, though, we don't need to know what gets left out.) This means some of your RAM is now unavailable—it's been occupied. This area taken by your System Software is often referred to as the **System Heap.**

"About This Macintosh" tells you how much RAM has been taken by System and Application software.

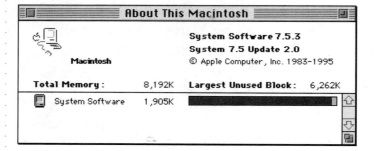

Try this: Restart your Mac while holding down your Shift key. This lets you avoid any goofy Extensions or Control Panels that might distort our discussion of how RAM works—we'll get to those later. Don't launch any of your application programs either.

See what is happening with the RAM by going to your Apple Menu and choosing **About This Macintosh.** First look at **Total Memory.** This is probably the most important item—it tells you how much RAM is physically installed in your computer. Now look at where it says **System Software.** The entire bar (including shaded and unshaded areas) shows how much has been "grabbed." Now check out the **Largest Unused Block;** it should roughly equal Total Memory minus System Software. "Largest Unused Block" tells you how much memory your application programs can use.

Notice how the bar indicating the System Software partition has two colored or shaded areas. The darker area on the left shows how much memory the System is actually using at that moment. The smaller area on the right is a buffer zone. It's RAM that has been taken by the System Software, but is not actually being occupied. Consider it to be an extra helping of RAM that the System holds in reserve, just in case. This gives the System some breathing room.

Application Partition

Let's launch an application. Use **Find File** to locate a program on your hard disk called "SimpleText." Almost every Macintosh has this basic word processing program loaded onto the hard disk—if you can't find it, almost any application should work for this example. Once you've tracked an application down, double-click to open it.

After it's launched, switch back to the Finder, go to your Apple Menu, and choose **About This Macintosh.** Notice how "Largest Unused Block" has been reduced by the same amount that SimpleText has grabbed—in this case 512K (shown below).

SimpleText also shows a two-shade partition in its bar. The area on the left indicates how much memory the application needs at this moment. The right-hand segment shows memory reserved for opening **additional** documents. Imagine you were going to write a bunch of long letters. As you created more and more files, the shaded area on the left would gradually fill in.

If you launch another program, say ClarisWorks, that program will take additional memory and reduce the "Largest Unused Block" even further.

SimpleText

You probably have several copies of SimpleText on your hard disk. Almost every time you install new software, another copy of SimpleText is also automatically installed.

 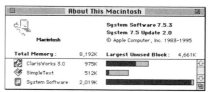

*"**About This Macintosh**" after launching SimpleText, (left) and then ClarisWorks (right).*

Keep launching program after program, and you will eventually run out of memory, getting a message telling you that you don't have enough RAM to launch this application.

What determines how much RAM area gets "grabbed" by an application? Why does SimpleText want 512K—especially since it apparently needs much less? **Get Info** gives us the answers.

Checking RAM Allocation with Get Info

If you quit SimpleText, you'll be able to control its **RAM allocation.** All you have to do is click *once* on the SimpleText application icon and use the **Get Info** command in the **File** menu. (If you don't see the Memory Requirements in the bottom left of the Get Info window, you didn't click on an *application.* Perhaps you clicked on a document or an alias—try again.)

You'll see three numbers in the Memory Requirements area in the bottom-right corner. These describe memory usage:

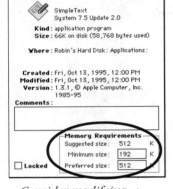

Consider modifying the Minimum and Preferred sizes on your favorite applications.

- **Suggested size:** This is what the people who wrote the program think is a safe yet reasonable compact amount of RAM that the program should have available. This number **cannot** be changed, and it has no effect whatsoever on how much memory is actually taken by the program. It is essentially just a guideline.

- **Minimum size:** This is what the programmers think is the minimum amount of RAM you should allocate to the program. More importantly, should you have only a minimal amount of RAM available (maybe you have lots of other programs running already) the program will launch, taking as little as that smaller amount, even though the suggested amount is not available. This number **can** be changed by you.

- **Preferred size:** This is how much RAM will be taken by the program if you launch it, assuming you have that much memory open. It also can be changed by you.

In plain English, SimpleText is saying: "I should have 512K dedicated to me. The very most I will take is 512K. If you don't have that much available, I will take as little as 192K, but no less." Given these settings, if you have only 267K available and open SimpleText, SimpleText will take **all** 267K, leaving absolutely no memory free.

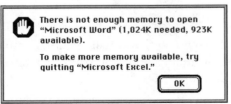

Have you seen this message before? It happens when you try to launch too many applications.

When and Why to Change the RAM Allocation

There are several good reasons why you should change the Minimum and Preferred RAM allocations. Here are the main things to consider.

Making Minimum and Preferred the Same is what I almost always do. It's the only way to make sure an absolute, certain amount of memory is given to a program.

Here's the problem: Let's say you have several applications running and you open PageMaker. It requires a minimum of 4250K and prefers 5250K. But you have something in between, like 4720K available: PageMaker takes all of it. This raises two issues: 1) PageMaker could do with less RAM allocated to it than you might think, and 2) every speck of RAM is now gone. With all RAM now taken, you're in dangerous territory. Sometimes your Mac will need just a little bit of free RAM to perform an operation (like printing), and it may freak out if you have absolutely no memory left.

Setting Minimum and Preferred to the same amount means the application will not launch unless this ideal amount is available.

I have PageMaker set to take 5250K of RAM, set in both Minimum and Preferred. This means PageMaker says to itself, "The programmers think I should have 4250K. I prefer to take 5250K, and I will *not* accept anything less."

Making Minimum and Preferred Larger than Suggested is a great idea if you have the space for it. This will generally make programs run more reliably and let you open more and larger documents. This extra breathing room often makes the program run faster too. Of course, this Preferred amount will only get grabbed if there's enough RAM installed or available for it.

Making Minimum and Preferred Smaller than Suggested may work for you if you absolutely must run more programs. If you're not opening many documents or particularly complex ones, this can let you squeeze in one more program. When you reduce the amount of RAM allocated to less than Suggested, you'll get a warning that it might cause the program to crash. As long as you're only setting a *little* less than Suggested, say 10 percent or so, you'll probably be okay. I still would do this only as a last resort.

The Best Scenario? Set Preferred a little more than Suggested, and make Minimum the same as Preferred.

The Problem of Fragmented RAM

Let's say you just got the error message telling you that you don't have enough memory to launch a program. Obviously, you need to quit something to free up RAM, so you quit one program. You try again, and still it won't run. Hmmm. You **quit** another program, try again, and you still don't have enough memory!

You check "About This Macintosh," and it tells you there's plenty of RAM open—so what the heck's going on?

Here's the story. Imagine memory is like a reservoir. It sits empty when the Mac is off. Turn it on, and it partially fills with your System software. Launch a program, say SimpleText, and it takes another segment that sits on top of the System segment.

Naturally, you're going to launch more programs than that, so after awhile you may have just about all the space occupied. So opening another program now will give you the old "not enough memory" message. Okay, so all the RAM is taken up, and you want to run Word. Word needs 1 megabyte (at least version 5.1 does), so you quit ClarisWorks. That's now more than 1 megabyte free, right? Wrong! You need **contiguous** free RAM; that is, the free RAM must be all together in one open chunk instead of split into little, disconnected pieces. **To defragment the RAM, quit everything and restart your Macintosh.**

*When you click in a close box, you are **closing the document— not quitting the application!***

Here's an 8MB RAM "reservoir" with System Software taking 2MB.

Open SimpleText, and another 512K is gone.

After running Claris- Works (1MB) and adding PageMaker to the mix (4MB), we now have less than 1MB of RAM left.

*Quitting ClarisWorks frees up RAM, but it is **discontiguous RAM**—it's broken into several pieces. Even though 1.8MB **total** is free, you **can't launch a program** if it wants more than one open "chunk."*

The Memory Control Panel

Virtual Memory

Starting with System 7, Apple implemented a new memory scheme called **Virtual Memory** (VM for short). Virtual Memory is special software that tricks your Mac into thinking some of your hard disk space is usable RAM. For many, the main benefit of using Virtual Memory is that you can run more programs.

Let's say you have 8 megabytes of RAM. If you turn on VM and you have at least 16 megabytes of unused *hard disk space,* you can "double" your memory—8 megabytes of "real," 8 megabytes of "false" hard-disk–based RAM. Don't set aside more virtual RAM than you have real RAM. That is, if you have 16 megs of real RAM, don't set aside more than 16 megs of your hard disk as virtual RAM or your Mac will run unreasonably slow.

Most Mac experts have abandoned the use of Virtual Memory as a way to run more programs. Instead, they use a program called **RAM Doubler** (see Chapter Seven). It's faster and easier.

Virtual Memory has become popular on **Power Macs,** though, as a way to significantly reduce the memory requirements of native applications (programs that have been written specifically for the Power Mac). Surprisingly, if you turn VM on, even just a little bit, many programs will require much less RAM.

The common strategy is to turn on VM so that your Power Mac has just one extra megabyte of virtual RAM. This gives you the benefit of programs that run leaner without taking much of a performance hit.

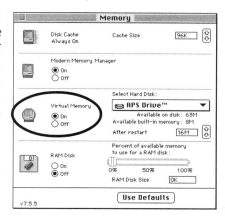

If you have a Power Mac, turn on Virtual Memory in the Memory Control Panel.

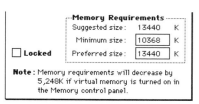

*Photoshop, like many applications, **requires far less memory** on Power Macs if VM is turned on— even just a little bit.*

Using the program RAM Doubler instead of Virtual Memory will give you this same benefit—Power Mac applications will need less RAM with RAM Doubler installed.

Disk Cache

Years ago, Apple came up with a scheme to make Macs faster. The idea is that upon startup, a certain amount of RAM can be set aside as a **cache.** This is memory that is "hidden" and cannot be used by your applications. With that cache set aside, your Mac starts keeping a close watch on what you constantly access from your hard disk.

Imagine that you regularly use the part of ClarisWorks that controls spell-checking. Since it's unusual for an entire program to be kept in RAM, the spell-checking part of ClarisWorks gets loaded into memory as needed and then discarded when it's not being used. That means if you're spell-checking several files, your Mac pauses to load that spell-checking "code" every time you hit the menu command to spell-check.

Your Mac will notice that this code keeps getting loaded and used, so it will decide to copy it into the **disk cache.** The next time you decide to spell-check, the Mac will instantly grab the spell-checking portion out of this reserved memory area rather than go find it on your hard disk and access it from there.

The idea is this: the larger your disk cache, the faster your Mac will run. Naturally, the downside is that you will have less usable memory for other stuff.

There is a great deal of debate over the value of this. It is well documented, for example, that perceptible speed improvements can be seen on a few models like the Mac IIci.

Many respected Mac gurus have specific amounts they set aside based upon how much RAM is installed. The figures usually thrown around are 32K per megabyte. So if you have 16 megabytes of memory, you'd set the disk cache to 512K (16 times 32).

My personal preference is to set the disk cache to its lowest possible level (32K). My reasoning is that the disk cache takes away from memory available to the programs, and I want my *programs* to have as much memory as they can get. Also, my experiments with varying disk cache settings have never resulted in a perceptible speed improvement. I prefer the concrete benefit of being able to run more programs over some nebulous speed improvement.

RAM Disk

Accessing something off of a disk will always be slower than grabbing it out of RAM. This was the original idea behind RAM disks. RAM disks "trick" your computer in a way that is totally opposite to what Virtual Memory does. Imagine making some of your *memory* think of itself as a *disk*. A RAM disk even shows up on the Desktop as an icon like a floppy disk or another hard disk!

Here's how some people use it:

They set a number in the Memory Control Panel for the size of a RAM disk—often enough megabytes to contain a small System Folder and an application. Then they restart. After the Mac **initializes** the RAM disk, a virtual disk icon appears on the Desktop.

Then they copy what they need into it. Maybe a nice, tiny System Folder from their Disk Tools disk (most Macintoshes come with one of these disks; see Chapter Four for more information) and an application folder, like a word processor.

Then they set the RAM disk as the startup disk and restart. Their Mac will restart very quickly, and their word processor will run really fast because there's no disk access involved. Everything the Mac needs is already in RAM!

In the old days, people used this strategy to make their Macs faster, especially before hard disks became affordable. Nowadays, it's the PowerBook users who want to save precious battery life. Since there's no disk drive needed, hence no motor to run, you can really prolong your battery life for those long flights.

One of the great things about the way RAM disks are handled by the Mac today is that a restart will no longer automatically remove the RAM disk—it can even endure some crashes. To get rid of it, you must throw away everything on the RAM disk, then go into the Memory Control Panel and turn it off.

RAM Disks—the wave of the future?

Considering that restarts are one of the most time-consuming things you do on your Mac and that RAM is getting pretty cheap these days, I can foresee a time when people put their entire System Folder on a permanent RAM disk.

I set up a 12MB RAM disk recently, and filled it with a System Folder loaded with Extensions and Control Panels. After making it the Startup

Disk, it took only **25 seconds** from hitting the Restart command to get the machine going. The little Extension icons that usually march across the bottom of my screen whizzed by! Compare this to the 30 seconds it took to start up from the hard disk with **no Extensions!**

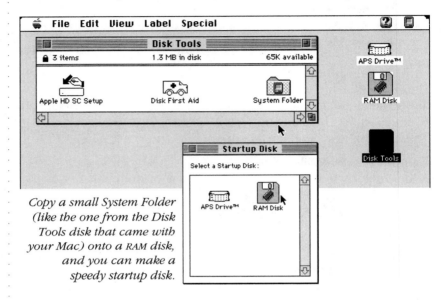

Copy a small System Folder (like the one from the Disk Tools disk that came with your Mac) onto a RAM disk, and you can make a speedy startup disk.

32-Bit Addressing

If you don't see "32-Bit Addressing" in your Memory Control Panel, don't worry about it.

If you have **8 megabytes of RAM or less** and "32-Bit Addressing" appears in your Memory Control Panel, turn it off.

If you have **8 megabytes of RAM or more** and "32-Bit Addressing" appears in your Memory Control Panel, turn it on. It's the only way you can actually *use* any RAM over 8 megabytes.

Modern Memory Manager

The "Modern Memory Manager" appears in Power Mac Memory Control Panels only. Power Macs handle memory differently from other Macs, and this difference can be a source of problems should you try to run programs in **Emulation mode** (see Chapter One). Normally this option should be On to get the best performance from your Mac. In rare instances where you are crashing while running older non-native programs, turning this off *may* solve the problem.

RAM Utilities

There are several third-party utilities specifically created for helping your Mac manage its RAM.

RAM Doubler

This program acts as a more efficient and easier-to-use version of Virtual Memory. I highly recommend it. For a complete description, see Chapter Seven.

Syncronys RAM Charger

When you first hear about how applications handle RAM you might say to yourself, "That's dumb—opening a program forces it to grab an absolute, fixed amount of memory, even if it actually needs much less? Why doesn't a program just take what it needs, and if it wants more, just ask for it?"

That's what RAM Charger from Syncronys allows you to do. It permits programs to dynamically give and take RAM. In conjunction with RAM Doubler, it can be a great way to maximize memory.

Unlike RAM Doubler or Virtual Memory, which expand memory, RAM Charger uses existing memory more effectively. It also differs from the other two memory-maximizing techniques in that *any* Mac running System 7 can use it. Even old Mac Pluses and SEs that can't run VM or RAM Doubler can run RAM Charger.

Important Things to Remember

- You can control an application's RAM usage using Get Info.
- Using Get Info to set Maximum and Preferred memory requirements for an application to the same number can be a very smart thing.
- Programs need contiguous free blocks of memory to run.
- Turning on a Power Mac's Virtual Memory will result in many programs requiring less RAM.
- A RAM disk can make a PowerBook's battery last longer, and can be used as a fast startup disk.
- RAM Doubler is generally a better "virtual memory" program than the one in the Memory Control Panel from Apple.
- Syncronys RAM Charger can make your Mac use RAM more efficiently.

Your Emergency Kit 4

The Big One is Coming

Living in Seattle, we are constantly warned that "The Big One is coming!" Of course, this refers to the big earthquake destined to shake us up within the next twenty years. My wife loves assembling and maintaining our earthquake preparation kit. We've got a tent, water, food, flashlights, candles, firewood, the whole nine yards. I'm glad she's on top of it, because I'd much rather spend my time prepping my Mac emergency kit.

Here's why I focus on the Mac: Unlike an earthquake, which can't reliably be predicted, I *know* that within the next three years there is a *99 percent* chance my Mac is going to freak out and be unusable for some reason.

Where did I come up with that figure? Simple. I made it up. Er— I mean, it comes from twelve years of professional computing experience, consulting with hundreds of Mac owners, and owning eleven Macs, with eighteen hard disks. Stuff just goes wrong!

Luckily, a Mac emergency kit is easy to assemble and provides immediate peace of mind. It's also a heck of a lot lighter than a big box of canned goods.

Here's the stuff you should have ready for that fateful day when your Mac goes haywire on you.

The All-Important Startup Disk

The most important item to have is a disk that can be used to **start up the Mac** in case your primary System Folder or the disk it's on dies. There are two big reasons why this is so important:

1. Some of the software programs that can prevent or repair damaged disks can't be used unless you start up from a disk other than the one that needs fixing/maintenance.

2. Your normal startup disk (usually the internal hard disk) may be unable to start up your Mac.

What we're talking about here is a disk that has a System Folder on it that your Mac can understand and use. Fortunately, your Mac came with one of these disks.

Disk Tools

Most Macs come with a Disk Tools disk that contains a minimal System Folder that can start up your computer.

Most Macs come with a set of floppy disks that allow you to reinstall your entire System Folder or run handy utility programs. Usually, this set of disks includes a floppy called the **Disk Tools** disk. This floppy is designed to start up your particular Macintosh model and may not work on a different Mac.

This disk contains a *minimal* System Folder, which means it's bare bones enough to run your Mac, but forget any software bells and whistles like printing or accessing a CD-ROM.

In addition to the System Folder, the typical Disk Tools disk has two pieces of diagnostic/repair software on it—**Disk First Aid** and **Apple HD SC Setup** or **Drive Setup**—which I discuss in more detail later.

Before you do anything else, find this disk (if you have one) and make a spare copy of it! Keep it handy, because you *will* need it someday. Or you can make your own disk (see next page).

If you have a **Performa** model Macintosh, look for a disk called "Disk Utilities." This also contains a stripped-down System Folder that can be used as a startup disk.

The Startup Disk Control Panel

If you have more than one disk with a working System Folder attached to your Mac, this terrific little utility allows you to tell your Mac which disk should "take charge" the next time you boot up the machine. Open and use this utility whenever you know you want

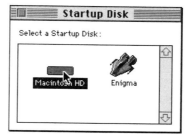

Startup Disk

Open the Startup Disk Control Panel to choose which disk takes control the next time you restart.

to start from another disk next time you boot. The other disk must be in or connected to the computer *before* you open this Control Panel.

Make your own Disk Tools floppy!

If you can't find a Disk Tools disk, check out the System CD that came with your computer. It may contain a file called **Disk Tools.image.** Double-click this to launch the program Disk Copy. After you click the "Make a Copy" button, it will prompt you to insert a blank floppy disk. Wait for a minute, and presto! You are now the proud owner of a Disk Tools disk.

If you don't have either of these disks or can't create the disk you need, don't fret. Your computer probably came with a CD you can use instead (next page).

On the System CD that came with your Mac is a "disk image" for a Disk Tools disk.

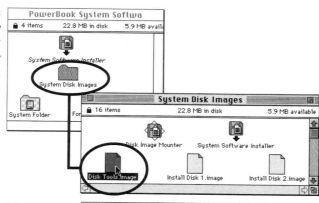

Double-click the "disk image" to launch Disk Copy, which will prompt you to insert a floppy disk.

Startup CD

If your Macintosh came with a CD-ROM drive, you probably have a CD that can be used to boot your Mac. Performa users should look for a disk called the **Macintosh Performa CD.** Regular Mac users will find the **Apple Macintosh CD.** Both of these CDs contain a fully functional System Folder *for the Mac model they came with*.

Usually (assuming your normal startup disk isn't working) you can:

- Just pop in the CD and restart to force the CD to take over.

- If that doesn't work, hold down the **C** key on the keyboard as the Mac restarts.

- If that doesn't work, hold down **Command Shift Option Delete** as the Mac attempts to boot up. This keyboard command is the "brute force" method for telling your Mac "Hey—ignore the System Folder in the internal hard disk, no matter what!" Naturally the only time you'd really use this shortcut is when you know that the external disk has a working System Folder on it.

The nice thing about using your CD-ROM disk for startup is that it contains a *significantly more functional System Folder than you get in the Disk Tools disk.* The bad news is that you can't put anything special on the CD that you want to run (like Norton Utilities or your favorite anti-virus program). Most folks just start up from the CD and pop in a floppy containing the other diagnostic/repair software they want to run.

External Hard Disk

External Removable Startup Disk

Many people use a variation of this technique by preparing a removable cartridge (Syquest cartridge, Zip disk, etc.) with a working System Folder on it.

I have a terrific way to ensure that a damaged System Folder doesn't slow me down for long: I have an external hard disk that plugs into the SCSI port in the back of my computer. Periodically (once a week or so) I drag my main System Folder (from the internal disk) over to the external disk to make a copy and in several minutes I have a backup of my entire folder.

Should something happen that makes the System Folder on my internal hard disk unusable, *I can just plug in the external device, restart, and the external hard disk will take command.* Then I simply replace the damaged System Folder by dragging the external backup over to replace it (assuming my internal *disk* is okay). This has saved my bacon about three times in the past couple of years.

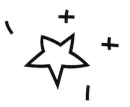

Complete System Install Disk(s)

All right—so you've prepared a disk that can be used to start up your Mac if need be. That gets you back up and running, but it may not get you back to **work.** You need the ability to create/recreate a full-featured System Folder.

Backup Files

As I just mentioned, the fastest and easiest way to recreate a working System Folder is to have a **duplicate of the one you use now** stored on an external hard disk or on a removable disk or cartridge.

This may not always be the perfect solution, because a recent backup might contain the same corruption that may be causing problems on your normal startup disk.

Another reason to have more than just the backup System Folder is if you need to install some component like a printer driver or something that isn't currently present in your folder or in the backup. For example, just the other day I needed the Easy Access Control Panel, and it wasn't in my System Folder or the backup folder. I grabbed my complete System install disk set and used the installer to grab just that component.

It's also good computer "hygiene" to periodically reinstall a complete System Folder from scratch.

What all this means is: find yourself a complete System Folder reinstall set of floppies or the CD.

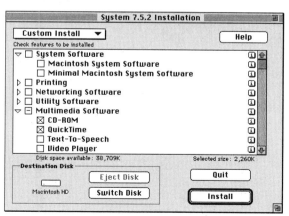

Using your System Install disk(s), you can choose to install single components of your System Software.

Install Floppies

If you already found a floppy called "Disk Tools," it was probably hanging out with other disks with names like "Install Me First" and "Goodies." These are the System install disks you want to keep around. In all likelihood, these are the disks that came with your Mac.

With these you could create a complete, fresh, rejuvenated System Folder that will work with your Mac on practically any hard disk.

Disk images

Has Apple gotten too cheap? On some newer Macs (like the Power-Book 5300 series) Apple saves themselves about ten bucks by putting **disk images** of the System install floppies on the internal hard disk.

To create floppy disks from the disk images, use the procedure I described earlier for creating a Disk Tools disk: Double-click on the disk image file to launch Disk Copy, and insert a blank floppy disk (that *you* supply). It copies all the files over that are needed on that particular disk, and will ask for new floppies as it needs them. After about twenty minutes you'll have a complete set of System install floppies.

If you can't find these disk images, look through your collection for a CD with the equivalent software on it.

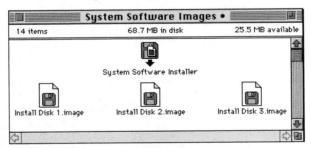

After spending a couple of thousand dollars for a PowerBook, Apple saved about ten bucks and made me create my own System install disks from these "disk images" on the hard disk.

Install CD

If your computer came with a CD-ROM drive, it probably also came with a CD that contains all the components needed to install the System software.

Regular, non–Performa-version Macintoshes have a CD called "Apple Macintosh CD" that permits you to install a complete System Folder in one of three ways:

1. **A pre-created System Folder** has been placed on the disk—mainly so the CD can act as a startup disk if necessary. You can drag wanted components right out of that folder onto a hard disk.

2. **A System installer and its related files** are present. Double-click the installer, and it will go through the motions to create a new System Folder from scratch.

3. **System install disk images** are used in conjunction with Disk Copy to create a complete set of System installation floppy disks.

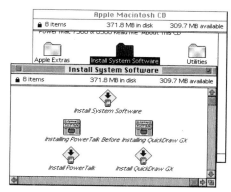

From a non-Performa Mac CD you can configure and install a complete new System Folder.

Performa Owners are given fewer options. The Macintosh Performa CD comes with:

1. **A pre-created System Folder**—it's an exact duplicate of the System Folder you found on your hard disk the first time you started up the Performa.

2. **A limited System installer** called Apple Restore, used to grab the files off the CD from the folder called "Restore System Folder." All this does is create a clone of the original Performa System Folder described above.

Wait! I Can't Find Any of these Disks!

*Call Apple's support line at **(800) SOS-APPL** to order a set of System install disks. Depending on your type of Mac and when you bought it, they will send you disks for a minimal cost (or sometimes for free!)*

An Ounce of Prevention...

In Chapter Five I discuss the important maintenance tasks that help keep your Mac healthy. Here are the programs you need to assemble to perform those disaster prevention activities.

Many of these utilities are shareware or freeware (also called "public domain" software), so you won't be able to buy them in a store or through mail order. You will be able to find them online through the Internet, America Online, or CompuServe.

Don't forget about your local Mac user group—they probably have a library of these files that you can access.

Disk First Aid

Every Mac owner gets **Disk First Aid** with their computer. I often describe it as "Norton Utilities, Jr." It does a respectable job of scanning disks for trouble and fixing the problems. It doesn't have all the bells and whistles of the commercial disk repair programs, but it's free, easy to use, and sometimes has been able to fix problems on my disks the expensive utilities couldn't.

The biggest problem with Disk First Aid is that **it can't repair the startup disk.** This is one of the main reasons you want it sitting on a startup floppy you've prepared. If you start your machine up from the floppy (Disk Tools) disk and run Disk First Aid from there, it'll work great.

 Some of the volumes you selected can't be repaired. You cannot repair the startup disk, the Disk First Aid disk, a write protected disk, a disk with open files, or any disk when File Sharing is active.

You may still verify these disks.

[OK]

Another reason to have a Disk Tools startup floppy. The Disk First Aid program can't fix your hard disk unless you start up from another disk.

Disinfectant

Disinfectant is a freeware program designed to seek out and destroy viruses. It scans your hard disk, tells you where the viruses are, and nukes 'em. It works great and the price is right. **Don't pay money for anti-virus software.** The commercial programs don't offer any significant benefit over Disinfectant.

Norton Utilities

Norton Utilities (from Symantec, $150) is the Big Kahuna of disk maintenance and repair programs. It can do a ton of useful things, such as repair damaged disks, recover trashed items, and defragment your hard disk.

I consider this to be an essential part of your maintenance tool kit, because it can catch minor hard disk problems early and fix them before they become major data-loss hassles.

PowerBook Owners Alert!

If you own a PowerBook 520 or 540, check your hard disk for two programs: an application called **Intelligent Battery Update** and an Extension called **Intelligent Battery.**

You should run the Intelligent Battery Update application monthly. You must have the Intelligent Battery *Extension* loaded as well for the *application* to work (restart with the Extension in the Extensions folder).

PowerBook 5300 users should run the **Battery Recondition** program that came with their computers monthly as well. Unlike the Intelligent Battery Utility, Battery Recondition doesn't require any special extension to be present.

Periodic corruption creeps in to your "intelligent" battery, making it stupid. This can cause overcharging and potential damage. If your PowerBook feels really hot on the bottom—you're overdue.

. . . A Pound of Cure

Taking preventative measures is important, but even the most rigorous maintenance schedule won't prevent all corruption, crashes, and hardware failure. Having the following goodies available will usually get you back up and running when things go wrong.

Backups

You knew this was coming right? I've said it before, and I'll say it again. **Back up your important data/disks frequently,** and keep them separate from the computer. This is crucial for one of two reasons— it can greatly streamline the repair process, or *it can replace the repair process altogether.* Often things cannot be fixed. In that case having a backup is your only hope of getting your work back.

An Extensions Manager

In Chapter Two I describe how using an extensions manager can assist in pruning your System Folder to usable proportions. Extensions managers can also be used to diagnose and even repair extension conflicts.

Apple's Extensions Manager

Apple's Control Panel, the one that comes with your computer, is easy and free. It's also pretty lame as a diagnostic/repair tool. If you suspect crashing or other problems are a result of conflicts, you must resort to manually turning on and off extensions and control panels, then restarting to see what happens. This has to be done repeatedly until you find out what programs aren't getting along.

Extensions are loaded in alphabetical order. But some extensions need to be loaded in a certain order, such as RAM Doubler, which needs to be loaded first. That's why there is a space at the beginning of RAM Doubler's name—it forces it to the top of the alphabetical list because spaces are sorted before letters. Other extensions (like Adobe Type Manager) put a tilde (~) at the beginning to force it to load last—the tilde comes after "z" in an alphabetical listing. Sometimes one Extension needs to be activated before another Extension can load properly.

But Apple's Extensions Manager is **unable to reorder** extensions. That is, it can't change the order in which they load. You have to do it yourself in the Finder by manually changing the name of the Extension or Control Panel.

Conflict Catcher—Longtime Favorite of the Experts

Until recently, Conflict Catcher (from Casady & Greene, $100) with all its capabilities was the features king of extension manager utilities. It pioneered several important diagnostic improvements over Apple's Extensions Manager.

Besides giving you the ability to set the order of extension loading, it can be told to **test for conflicts**. When you instigate the testing process, Conflict Catcher will turn off extensions one by one and restart with various combinations until it identifies the culprit(s). It then prompts you, asking if you want to try reordering them. It will then test some new ordering schemes to see if any cure the problem.

Now Startup Manager 7.0—The New Contender

Now Startup Manager version 7.0 (from Now Software, $49) is an updated version with some enhancements that claim to match (if not beat) Conflict Catcher's features. Sure, it's got the automatic reordering options, as well as automated testing.

What's been added is a link from the manager to a database of known Extension and Control Panel conflicts. This database is called the "Now Startup Manager Reference Library" and is a file that sits on your hard disk. The Startup Manager accesses it to make sure you haven't installed extensions or control panels that are known to fight with each other. This database file is updated monthly; version 7.0 users can download the latest library from Now Software's Web site (http://www.nowutilities.com).

Disk First Aid

Not only valuable for preventing problems, Disk First Aid is also a good disk and file fixer. See page 90.

Norton Utilities

Norton Utilities is the first thing I run when a disk or file is acting flaky. Norton Utilities contains three programs for fixing problems:

1. **Norton Disk Doctor:** NDD looks for damage on disks and if it finds problems, asks you if you want to fix them. This is the most important component.

2. **Volume Recover:** Volume Recover can work all by itself to repair individual damaged files. In addition, if you had installed Norton's FileSaver Extension prior to experiencing problems, Volume Recover can work in conjunction with the extension to fix things that Norton Disk Doctor can't.

    (Personally, the last thing I want is another darned extension to worry about, so instead, I keep frequent backups in case Disk Doctor doesn't work.)

3. **UnErase.** If you threw something in the Trash, emptied the Trash, have no backup, and want it back again, this program may be able to retrieve it.

The reason you can sometimes get files back from the Trash is that **trashed files are not immediately erased!** I'll bet you thought throwing something in the Trash and emptying it scrubs the item off your disk, right? No, no, no! All the computer does is make that space on your disk "available" for something new to move in.

Think of your disk as an apartment building. When you empty the Trash, it's like telling the apartment manager (the System and Finder) that this tenant (the trashed file) is all set to move out and to take its name off of the tenant directory by the front door. It's like putting out a For Rent sign. A new tenant (file) can occupy that space anytime the manager feels like putting somebody in there.

But if you go upstairs to the apartment and open the door, the old "tenants" are still there—nobody knows it because the tenant directory says they're gone. Once the manager decides to move in a replacement tenant (a new file) the original "tenant" is then replaced and gone forever. Since your hard disk has thousands of "apartments" called "sectors," a new file might not move into that recently vacated space. A trashed file could stay on your disk for a few minutes, or a few months.

Programs like Norton UnErase have caused untold embarrassment for people like Ollie "I thought I trashed that e-mail" North, and Bryant "I thought those nasty memos about my coworkers were gone" Gumbel.

Here's a tip if you decide to sell your Mac and don't want people to resurrect your sensitive data (and you don't want to buy an expensive security program):

1. **Toss everything but the System Folder and one other big application folder into the Trash.** The Photoshop folder, the Word folder, or the ClarisWorks folders are good choices to keep (make sure there isn't anything inside this folder that you want to keep secret.)

2. **Empty** the Trash.

3. **Select the one saved application folder** and choose the **Duplicate** command from the File menu. It will make a copy.

4. **Drag the original application folder into the duplicate folder.** This creates a folder twice as large as the original.

5. **Duplicate this new folder** and move the previous folder into it. You'll be doubling the size again.

6. **Repeat this sequence** of duplications and moves, until your Mac gives you an error saying there isn't enough room on the disk to make another duplication.

7. **Open this big folder.** View the contents By Date. The most recent duplicate is at the top of the list. Choose that most recent folder and duplicate it one more time, right there in the folder. Now close that folder.

8. **Drag this big folder into the Trash** and empty the Trash. Should anyone try to resurrect your data, all they'll find is ClarisWorks or Photoshop repeated over and over.

Disk Formatting/Driver Software

This is one of the most important things to stay on top of, yet few people seem to talk about it. When a hard disk starts acting flaky, the **driver** software may be corrupted or incompatible. Very often replacing or updating this software can solve the problem.

A disk driver is the software that acts as a link between your System Folder and the hard disk itself. Think of it this way—the System and Finder talk to the driver software, and the driver talks to the disk. Like any piece of software, this file can be damaged. Here are the programs you can use to install a fresh driver.

Apple HD SC Setup

Drive Setup

Your Disk Tools disk has either Drive Setup or Apple HD SC Setup on it. These can be used to reinstall your hard disk driver software.

If your hard disk came from Apple:

Life used to be so easy (before 1995). If you bought a Mac with a hard disk, it came with a program called **Apple HD SC Setup.** Any Mac with an Apple hard disk could have the driver updated with this software. Although *some* new Macs can use this same program today, most newer models must use a different program called **Drive Setup.**

The easy way to find out which one is the best for you to use is to check out the **Disk Tools** disk that came with your machine (or create this disk from a disk image file as described earlier in this chapter, page 85). It will have a copy of the appropriate software.

If your hard disk did not come from Apple:

Neither Apple HD SC Setup nor Drive Setup can be used to install a driver onto a non-Apple hard disk.

Luckily, *all third-party hard disks ship with their own driver installing program.* Some of the more popular ones include programs like **APS Power Tools, Silverlining,** or **Hard Disk ToolKit.** Look for a floppy disk that came with your hard disk. It will contain the software. No floppy? Check the hard disk itself.

If you want to do what many pros do:

The Mac gurus I know, particularly those who have to keep many different Macintoshes up and running, buy a good commercial hard disk utility like **Drive 7** (Casa Blanca Works, $80) or **Silverlining** (La Cie, $150).

The nice thing about buying one of these programs (and making sure you update it periodically) is that you can rest assured it will work on *all* Macs and all disks.

Reformatting the Hard Disk

The programs just described (Apple HD SC Setup, Drive Setup, APS Power Tools, Silverlining, Drive7, and Hard Disk ToolKit) can do a lot more than just install drivers. *They can also reformat the hard disk.* During reformatting, the hard disk is totally erased and new magnetic "trails" are laid down to guide files to where they should be saved.

> **Danger!** Reformatting erases *everything*—and in many cases irretrievably. **Reformat the hard disk only when you give up** and decide that the data on the disk is lost forever. Reformatting will wipe the disk clean of all data.
>
> The point is: *Don't reformat when all you need to do is replace the driver.* Fortunately, all of these programs make it very clear when you're going to do something dangerous.

SCSIProbe-3.5

SCSIProbe

If you have a hard disk, removable cartridge, or CD-ROM that refuses to show up on the Desktop, the SCSIProbe Control Panel (pronounced "scuzzy probe") will usually force it to appear. All you do is launch SCSIProbe and click the "Mount" button. Nine times out of ten the problem disk will show up.

			SCSIProbe-3.5	
			SCSIProbe 3.5sq	
ID	Type	Vendor	Product	Version
0	DISK	IBM	H3171-S2	S61D
1	ROM	NEC	CD-ROM DRIVE :500	2.5
2	CPU	HP	C1750A	3125
3				
4				
5	DISK	QUANTUM	LIGHTNING 730S	241E
6	DISK	IOMEGA	ZIP 100	L.27
7	CPU	APPLE	Jeff Carlson	$077D

Update   Mount   Options...

CanOpener

Twice a year I get a call from some hapless QuarkXPress, Word, or PageMaker user. They say "Steve! My Mac says that the newsletter I've been working on for the past week is corrupted and cannot be opened! This thing is due at the printer tomorrow!"

Now you know what I say—"No problem, just open one of the **back-ups** you've made and update it." But most of the time they have no reasonable backup file, and often we can't repair the damage. All is not lost, however.

The program **CanOpener** (Abbott Systems, $65) **can look into the document and extract the data from it.** While **it can't fix the file** so you can reopen it, it can extract the text and images out of the file so you can try to reassemble it in a new document. It's not a perfect solution, but it can often save hours or even days of work.

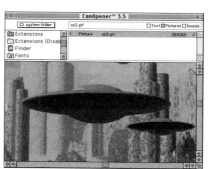

This is CanOpener extracting a graphic out of a corrupted document.

Important Things to Remember

- Backup your hard disk.
- Find or make a Disk Tools disk.
- Find or make System install disk(s).
- Buy Norton Utilities.
- Get an extensions manager or learn to use Apple's Extensions Manager.
- Find the hard disk formatting software that came with your Mac, or buy a program like Drive7 or Silverlining.

Important Rituals

5

An Ounce of Prevention . . .

Most people change the oil in their car regularly, visit the dentist twice a year, and get an annual physical. What most Mac users don't realize is that they must be just as diligent about the mandatory Macintosh maintenance rituals to prevent mayhem and inconvenience down the road.

So, we talked about the software and hardware you need in your emergency kit—now let's talk about how to *prevent* emergencies with these tools.

Incremental Backups

You already know you should backup the contents of your hard disk regularly. How often you do that is up to you, but most experienced users agree there shouldn't be more than a week between backups. Here are a few tips to make the process easier.

Documents Folder

One technique for an easy backup is to save all the documents you create into a single folder. Then all you have to do is copy that one folder and all of your important work is backed up.

For many years, Performa owners have had a neat feature to force all files to be saved into a Documents folder, making it easy to ensure complete backups. Systems 7.5 and 7.6 now include this feature for all Macs:

Documents

Go to your **General Controls** Control Panel. You'll see an option to save your documents to a Documents folder. If you don't already have a Documents folder, the Mac will make one for you and put it on the Desktop. From then on, every time you save a document it will automatically go into this folder.

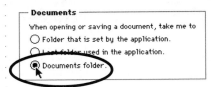

You can use your General Controls Control Panel to force all the documents you create to go to a Documents folder.

While most power users forgo this option, new Mac users can take advantage of this single-folder solution to make it easy to copy all their work to a single floppy or cartridge.

This is a great way to go if you have a pretty new Mac and haven't created many documents—odds are you could drag your entire Documents folder to a single floppy disk and it would all fit. The hassles begin when you need more than one floppy disk, or if you have a file larger than 1.4 megabytes. At that point you need to escalate to a more sophisticated system, such as using a cartridge or external hard disk and/or backup software.

Use the Find File Feature for Backing Up

You can use the **Find File** feature to find files that have changed within a given time period, then copy all of them to a floppy disk (or other disk). You might have tried before to look for files that have changed within a certain period.

1. At the Desktop, press Command F to bring up Find File (or choose Find File from the Apple menu).

2. In the first option, choose to find items by "date modified." In the middle area choose the "is" option. In the third area specify today's date.

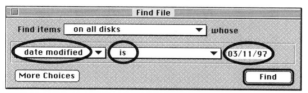

It's easy to make Find File find things that have changed today.

This will return a pretty long list that may include some unwanted finds (like applications and the cache files your Web browser may have stored on your hard disk).

3. Click the "More Choices" button to bring up additional search criteria—this extra criteria can be used to limit the number of found files. You might try to specify a second request where the "kind" is "document," but even then you'll probably encounter too many items. So:

What's neat is that you can specify files *created by a certain application.* In the criteria option for your second choice, choose "creator." Then if you know the four-character **creator code** for that application, you can just specify that code as your limiting criteria. The problem is these codes aren't easy to find unless you know the trick.

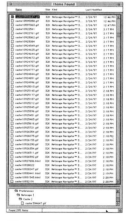

The problem with using only the "date modified" criteria is that you find a lot of things you don't want to backup.

4. Most Macintoshes have special drag-and-drop software installed as part of their System software. This means you can drag a sample file into the Find File window to specify a creator code! Try it. If you want to find Word documents, drag a Word document to Find File and drop it into the space for the third option, as shown below. Now Find File will find all files created by that application!

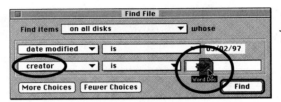

It's great—drag a file into the Find File window to set an example of what you want to search for.

5. After the find is complete, choose the "Select All" command under the Edit menu. This will highlight all the found items and you can drag them all to a floppy disk or cartridge.

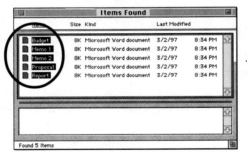

Use the "Select All" command to grab all the found items—now you can drag them to another disk for copying.

You can use this drag-and-drop technique in conjunction with the Documents folder. If your entire Documents folder can't fit on a floppy disk, try this:

Ask Find File to look for items whose modification date is "today." Then drag the Documents folder onto the "Find items" menu (shown below). This forces Find File to look only in the Documents folder! It will ignore all the other items on your hard disk that have changed.

Drag a folder or even a disk to the "Find items" menu to force it to search only within that location.

Another Cool Incremental Backup Tip

Another use for labels!

1. Open your **Labels** Control Panel and make a label called "Backup."

2. Mark your important day-to-day items (calendar, checkbook, phone list, etc.) with that label.

3. On those days when you're not doing a real backup, use Find File to locate those labeled items, then copy them to one or more floppies.

   a. If the files are too large to fit on a floppy disk, make a folder on the Desktop.

   b. Copy the files into that folder (Option-drag to make the copies).

   c. Finally, run Disk Doubler or some other compression program on that folder—this may shrink things down to a manageable size.

Backing Up with Backup Software

Performa owners get a free backup program called **Apple Backup** that will duplicate files onto a series of floppy disks automatically. The program just asks you to insert one disk after another until the job is complete. It will split large files into parts that will fit onto several disks. If your hard disk dies later, you simply install a whole new drive mechanism and run the backup program again, this time reversing the procedure by *restoring* the data. This time it asks you to insert the backup floppies one at a time until all the files are copied back onto the new disk—it even makes identical folders and locations for the files as on the original hard disk. This procedure is pretty simple to use, but time-consuming. Robin tested it a while ago—it took 6 hours and gobbled up 117 disks!

Most experts prefer the commercial backup programs **Diskfit** or **Retrospect** to accomplish the task of backing up a lot of data. Retrospect will allow you to back up onto a tape drive as well.

Tape is neat because the media is inexpensive (data tapes resemble audio cassette tapes), and a single tape can hold hundreds of megabytes of data. Network administrators swear by this backup method. It allows machines to be backed up at night over the network to a central Mac with a tape drive without anyone even being there!

Rebuild the Desktop

As Robin says in *The Little Mac Book*, rebuild the Desktop file at least once a month. I have to admit that I do it weekly, but I'm a little more paranoid. Hold down the Command and Option keys at startup and keep them held down until you see the dialog box prompting you to rebuild the Desktop file.

To keep your windows opening fast and your icons looking right, rebuild once a month.

Forward

*A blank icon like this, when you **know** it is supposed to have an image of some sort, can indicate that it's time to rebuild the Desktop.*

Not only does rebuilding the Desktop make your windows open and close faster, but it can also kill certain kinds of viruses. If some of your icons look generic (they lose the details that make it obvious which application they are or link to), you're overdue for a rebuild.

Rebuilding without restarting

To rebuild the Desktop without restarting, force-quit the Finder (press Command Option Escape). Hold down Command and Option as the Finder launches again.

Scan Your Hard Disk for Problems

Most people wait until something goes wrong before they run Disk First Aid or Norton Utilities. The experts run one or both of these programs monthly—*before* trouble crops up.

Scan for Viruses

Viruses get blown way out of proportion in the media as far as being a threat to your data. Most Mac viruses are created with the simple goal of multiplying, not for searching out your data and destroying it. I personally don't know anyone on a Macintosh who has lost a single file from a viral infection. (Viruses *are* a more serious problem on PCs, however, which is another point in the Mac vs. PC debate.)

Nonetheless, Mac viruses can be troublesome pests that cause crashes and other odd behavior, so you'll want to eradicate them.

Disinfectant

Disinfectant is the antiviral software of choice. It's fast, it's complete, and best of all it's free (get it online or from your local user group). Run it monthly. It will scan your disks for infection and will kill all viruses it finds. Even though Disinfectant can create an Extension that will automatically scan floppies for viruses, your System Folder already has too much stuff in it!

Disinfectant

Paying money for anti-virus software?

Symantec AntiVirus for the Macintosh (SAM), Virex, and other commercial applications exist to eradicate viruses. I have used them all and have not found a compelling reason for choosing any of them over Disinfectant.

Defragment Your Hard Disk

You've seen the ads—they tell you how your files scattered in pieces all over your hard disk really slow things down. You need to defragment the disk to ensure that all your applications and documents are in contiguous areas (areas touching each other). Defragmenting also reduces wear and tear on the drive mechanism. I've even heard claims that it will free up space on the hard disk.

In theory all this makes perfect sense. Unfortunately, perceptible speed improvements from defragging are nonexistent in the real world. Fragmentation is simply not the problem the software companies would have you believe. The last time I ran one of these defragmenters I got 14K freed up (K not MB!).

The scary thing is that if you experience a crash, power failure, or other mishap (someone trips over the power cord) while the defragging is in progress, you can lose the contents of the entire hard disk.

The only folks I can recommend this procedure to are professional Photoshop users who need contiguous free space for the Photoshop virtual memory scheme called the "scratch disk."

The Bottom Line: Your Ritual Schedule

Okay, so when and how often do we do all these things? Which ones are the most important?

Here is my suggested list of tasks and times in order of importance:

1. **Backup:** Do it daily or weekly, depending on how critical your data is.

2. **Rebuild the Desktop:** Once a week.

3. **Run Disk First Aid** or commercial disk repair software: Once a month.

4. **Run Disinfectant:** Once a month.

These are important things. Staying on top of them will make your Mac much happier. While doing these rituals can't prevent all potential problems, they will help keep your data safer and ultimately make your life easier!

Disaster Recovery   6

Troubleshooting

Oh, sure, the Mac is the easiest computer in the world to use—but that doesn't mean it's going to run forever without having some kind of time-consuming problem. Computers are supposed to be these great labor-saving devices, but after I've spent an afternoon trying to figure out why the darn thing won't work, I sometimes wonder if all the time gained from using a computer gets evaporated by dealing with technical glitches. Fortunately, knowing some of the more useful troubleshooting techniques can often get you back to work in no time.

This chapter is designed to get you on the fast track to problem-solving. We're going to discuss the most common problems, how to prevent them, and the fastest ways to solve them.

We don't have the space here to cover all the hardware and software maladies possible. For an exhaustive reference guide to almost any Mac problem and its solution, get *Sad Macs, Bombs, and Other Disasters,* by Ted Landau, available from Peachpit Press. Ted is the most knowledgeable guru I know of when it comes to troubleshooting Macs, and his book is terrific.

Here are the most important troubleshooting things to consider.

Prevent Trouble

Keep frequent backups

We've beat this one to death in the previous chapters, *but making a backup is still the most important thing you can do*. Not only is it important for when you lose everything on your hard drive, but it's the handiest technique for replacing corrupted programs and documents.

Resist change

As someone who loves this crazy, constantly changing world of high-tech, I feel strange suggesting that change is bad. But it is. Installing new software (and hardware) is fraught with danger.

Naturally, if you don't have a spreadsheet program and you just bought Excel, you need to install it. The same is true if you've been using Photoshop 3.0 and want to take advantage of the new features of 4.0. What I'm *discouraging* is the knee-jerk reaction of many computer users to upgrade software just because there's any kind of updated version.

Here are some things to consider when you're going to install the latest and greatest update of (insert software name here):

- This new version will be slower than the version you have now. All software companies claim their latest and greatest version has "several speed enhancements" that are supposed to make it faster—don't believe it. Sure, they can often make a few isolated operations faster, but if they've added features, the program as a whole is slower.
- It requires more RAM and disk space.
- It will toss random items into your System Folder that are practically guaranteed to cause some degree of mayhem.
- You probably haven't touched 80 percent of the features of the version you have installed now. Why do you need something new?
- Does this new product have a compelling benefit— does it let you do something you couldn't do before?
- Your computer probably runs okay now. Do you want to mess with something that works?
- Upgrading costs money.

Taking that information into account, most of the upgrading people do is frivolous. Here's an example that comes to mind. My Mac was running great when someone in the office noticed I was running a slightly out-of-date version of the Mac System software. Apparently an update had been issued that would fix bugs and add some speed improvements.

Despite my protestations, my overzealous coworker plopped in an update disk, ran the updater, and restarted my machine. As the computer came back to life, I got a System Error. We tried again. Another System Error.

Rather than get into three hours of troubleshooting, I simply hooked up my backup disk, copied a replacement System Folder over the now-damaged one, and was back in business. True, a half-hour of my life was irretrievably lost, but it could have been much worse.

I have dozens of examples of coworkers and clients installing gratuitous new software only to face hours or even days of frustration and lost time. One of the most productive Mac users I know is running a System and application suite that's three years old. He rarely crashes, and he gets more done than 99 percent of folks who have the latest and greatest software.

Perform the Important Rituals

As mentioned in Chapter Five, rebuilding the Desktop, running Disk First Aid, making regular backups, and an occasional cleansing with Disinfectant will help keep you in good shape.

Conflicts

Most problems you encounter on your Mac are caused by conflicting applications, Control Panels, and Extensions. Many of these hassles can be bypassed by judicious pruning of your System Folder, as described in Chapter Two.

Hardware

Although it can take a while, your hardware can and will eventually go bad on you.

Usually your hard disk will go first, as it's one of the only things in the computer with moving parts. There are lots of little things that can go bad—a belt can break, the motor can fail, or a ball bearing can wear out. Unfortunately, when a small part on a hard drive fails, the repair people always replace the entire drive mechanism. They claim it's less expensive to toss out the whole thing and replace it than to go in and take the time to repair a small, hard-to-find component.

Luckily, hard drives are relatively cheap these days, and replacing them is easy. As long as you keep frequent backups, you'll be in pretty good shape.

Corruption

Here's a more elusive yet pervasive culprit. Corruption is an insidious problem that can affect just about anything on your disks. Here's how it usually plays out:

You're working on a report, and just as you hit the Save command, there's a power failure. When the power returns, you restart the machine and try to open the report again. Boom! A System Error.

You restart again, try to open the file, and the same thing happens. Your report is damaged. The file on the hard disk has been corrupted and may never open correctly again.

It's not only files that are affected—your *applications* can be corrupted as well. *In fact, nothing on your disk is immune* from this problem. You don't even need a power failure for this thing to happen. One of the most vexing problems is that of font corruption. A corrupted font in your System Folder can cause any and all applications to crash. Luckily most of the font management programs discussed in Chapter Ten can root them out.

File, font, and application corruption can happen all by itself. The only easy solution for this kind of thing is (you guessed it) to keep frequent backups.

Viruses

Viruses can corrupt files. Rarely do they seek out and destroy data on purpose, but they often cause subtle corruption of applications and documents as a by-product of their reproduction. Run Disinfectant at least once a month.

Startup Problems

I hate when this happens. You come into the office in the morning, turn on the machine, go get a cup of coffee, and when you come back—the Mac's not running!

This is the kind of problem that could either take two minutes to solve or has the potential to cause a whole day of downtime. Here's what can go wrong:

Chimes of Doom

If you turn on your Mac, hear a weird set of tones you've never heard before, and see the poor, dead Mac on your screen, you may have a hardware problem.

SCSI conflict

SCSI (Small Computer Systems Interface) is the data transfer bus that most hard disks and scanners connect to (see Chapter One for a more complete description).

The dead Mac could mean a bad SCSI connection or something much worse—hardware failure.

(Here's something spooky: this file had corruption problems and I was able to trace it to this graphic of the dead Mac. Aaiieee!)

The Chimes of Doom are often caused by SCSI connection problems. To see if this is the case, begin by unplugging everything from the SCSI port and restarting. Usually doing that will at least let you get going again. If you can start your Mac without any SCSI devices attached, that's a clue that the problem is probably with one of the SCSI connections. Shut down and:

- Check to make sure every SCSI device has a different address (see Chapter One about SCSI addresses).

- Make sure the correct device is properly *terminated* (see Chapter One). Proper SCSI termination is very important.

- Try new or different cables on a bad connection. SCSI cables should be as short as possible, and make sure they don't twist.

- Plug devices back in one at a time, restarting after each new connection.

- Try connecting the cables to different ports (the left one instead of the right one, or the upper one instead of the bottom one). It doesn't seem like it should make a difference, but it can. Remember, this is voodoo.

Bad system software

If unplugging SCSI stuff has no effect, attempt a restart with a Disk Tools disk from your emergency kit (Chapter Four). This may not have any effect in itself, but if it works it indicates that reinstalling your System software could solve the problem.

Hardware failure

If neither of these approaches work, you need to get the computer into the repair shop because something is broken!

The Dreaded Blinking Question Mark

Only slightly less disconcerting than the Chimes of Doom is the dreaded blinking question mark. It means the computer is having some kind of problem finding or working with your System Folder. Here's what could be happening:

Your Mac wants to know: Where the heck is the System Folder?

SCSI problem

It could be that some kind of SCSI interference is preventing the Mac from seeing your startup disk. Turn the machine off, unplug all SCSI devices (unless your startup disk is an external SCSI drive, of course!), and restart. If you still see the blinking question mark, your System Folder could be damaged.

Damaged System Folder Item(s)

When corruption affects your System file (the "System" program that lives in the System Folder), the Finder file, or an Enabler, the blinking question mark can result. Once again, the Disk Tools disk comes to the rescue (see Chapter Four on where to find the disk).

These are the System and Finder icons.

Pop in the Disk Tools disk, and you should see a "Happy Mac." Hopefully, when you get into the Finder, your startup hard disk will appear automatically as a mounted volume (that is, its icon will show up on the Desktop.) If the hard disk **does** appear without any problem, something is probably wrong in your System Folder (the computer should **not** ask if you want to initialize the disk, for example).

At the very least, you need to replace the System file and/or the Finder. At most, the entire System Folder may need replacing.

You might be tempted to replace the damaged ones by dragging copies of the System and Finder from the Disk Tools floppy into the System Folder on the hard disk. **Don't do it.** The System and Finder that are on the floppy are minimized to use less disk space, and are

If a Disk Tools floppy is inserted before startup, it will boot your computer and take command.

not designed for handling a major System Folder with lots of Control Panels and Extensions.

See page 44 for information about Enabler files.

Dragging the System, Finder, and Enabler files *from a recent backup* is the easiest and fastest way to "rejuvenate" a damaged System Folder. If you're like me and back up your entire hard disk onto an external hard drive, Syquest cartridge, or Zip disk, replacing these files is easy: shut down the Mac, hook up the drive, and restart. The backup drive's System Folder will take over, and you'll soon be in the Finder.

If you don't have a backup System Folder to access, check out the CDs that came with your Mac. All Performas and some Power Macs come with a CD that contains a complete System Folder, identical to the one that was installed on the hard disk when you bought the machine. In many cases, you can boot from this CD and just drag the files over to the "bad" System Folder on your hard drive.

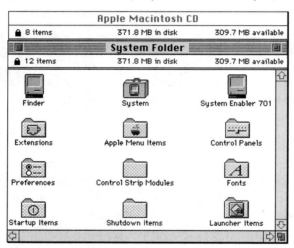

You can transplant certain items from the System Folder that lives on the CD that comes with most Macs.

Beware: If you have upgraded your System software since you purchased the computer (perhaps your Mac came with System 7.1 installed, and you upgraded it to version 7.5), then you can't use this technique of transplanting items from the original CD —you'll be putting an old System and Finder into a System Folder that wants a newer version, and you'll be in worse shape than before.

I do not generally recommend replacing the entire System Folder because your Preferences, Control Panels, and other items that may have been installed in the folder since the last backup **will be erased.** However, should the replacement of the System, Finder and Enabler not cut it, it's time to try replacing the entire folder.

What if you don't have recent copies of your System and Finder? How can you create a fresh System Folder and still keep your current Extensions, Control Panels, and Prefere·ices?

You need to have a set of **System install disks.** Most Macs come with a set of floppy disks or a CD that contains all the files needed to create a System Folder from scratch.

If you don't have a System install CD or disks, you'll need to order a set from Apple. Call their 800 number (1-800-SOS-APPL) and they can steer you in the right direction. Another route is to try a local dealer, your local Mac user group, or perhaps you know someone who can lend you a set.

To reinstall with the System install disks:

1. Insert the CD or the floppy disk labeled "Install Disk 1." Restart. You should now get the "Happy Mac," and in a minute you'll be up and running in the Finder. It will look different from what you are accustomed to because it is not *your* Finder that is running the Desktop, it is the Finder on the floppy disk or CD.

2. Go to the hard disk where your damaged System Folder is and **rename the System Folder.** I usually call it "Old System Folder." For good measure, I also drag out the System file and either trash it or give it a different name. This will make it impossible for your System Install program to think your goal is to update the existing System Folder. Instead it will think you have no System Folder at all and will create a new one.

3. Next, open the Installer program (double-click its icon) from the inserted disk. By default, the Installer program will want to do an **Easy Install,** which will assemble a System Folder that has the components Apple feels are appropriate for your Mac. Go ahead and use **Easy Install.**

You can trash your System suitcase file and rename the System Folder so the System Installer can't "see" it.

4. After your Mac goes through the installation process, restart without the CD or Install disk inserted. You should be back in business.

(If you still see a blinking question mark or fail to get to the Finder, *your hard disk is probably damaged*. See the following pages.)

5. Assuming you are up and running, it's now time to surgically implant your old System Folder contents and see if you can get back to status quo. First, open your old Preferences folder and move the Preferences into the new folder. *Avoid reinstalling old items that are copies of the new Preference items*—no sense installing an old preference that may be damaged.

Restart. You should be okay.

6. Then drag your old Control Panels folder **contents** into the new folder. Again, only install items that are different from the ones already present.

Restart.

7. Do the same with your Extensions. Restart (and cross your fingers). Odds are that you are now back where you should be, and you can get back to work.

However, if you get a System Error after any of the last three steps, it means one of your Control Panels or Extensions is damaged, or maybe something conflicts with another Extension. **Restart with the Shift key down to stop all Extensions and Control Panels from loading,** then try to find the culprit and remove it. (See page 120 for more info on how to do this.)

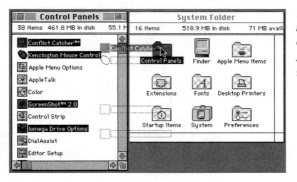

You can drag some of the old System Folder Control Panels and Extensions into the new System Folder.

Damaged hard disk

When you start up from the Disk Tools disk, your Mac may ask you if you want to initialize the hard disk. This is a mixed blessing. It's a good sign because the Mac still sees that the disk exists, but it's also a bad sign because it implies the disk has some major problems. Whatever you do, **don't initialize the disk!** *Initializing the hard disk will erase the entire thing.*

Try using **Disk First Aid** to repair the disk (see Chapter Two if you don't know where your Disk First Aid is). It may be able to fix the problem. If Disk First Aid cannot, try using a commercial disk repair program such as Norton Utilities.

Disk First Aid

Disk First Aid can fix many common problems.

Don't click "Initialize"! You need to run Disk First Aid instead.

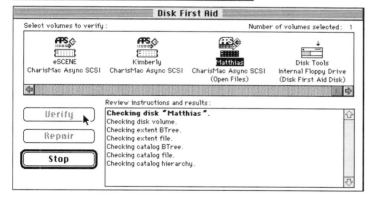

Dead hard disk

It could be that you popped in a CD or floppy with a System Folder on it, and when you restarted your hard disk never appeared on the Desktop. This is a bad thing. It probably means something is physically wrong with the disk.

Sometimes running the program **Disk First Aid** will help. It may tell you that it saw a problem and fixed it. It could be that all you have to do is restart. Maybe.

Most likely, Disk First Aid will say that there is no hard disk at all, or that the disk is damaged and it cannot fix the problem.

If it says there is no disk at all, many people say it's time to go to the repair shop. Bear in mind that the guys in the repair shop will *always say that the disk is hosed,* and they'll gladly install a new one at an inflated price (on top of the charge to diagnose the bad disk).

Here's what to do. If you have a Mac whose case can be opened, open up the computer. Clean out all the dust. Tighten the cable connections. Try again to start the computer. If the hard disk still fails, try this long shot:

Hard disks are sometimes afflicted with "sticktion." The motor can get old and so weak it doesn't have the torque to get the disk spinning without some help. Sometimes it can be jarred back into action. With the computer still plugged in, keep it level and give it a quick twist—jerk it about 180 degrees clockwise. If that doesn't work, try jerking it counterclockwise. Sometimes the hard disk will start spinning. Even if it works, this solution is short term at best. *Backup the disk instantly* and *immediately* plan on replacing it. Don't turn it off until you've backed it up.

Okay, let's say none of this works, and you need to replace the entire hard drive. Rather than pay through the nose, pick up a copy of *MacUser, MacWEEK,* or *Macworld* magazines, find a mail-order hard disk company in the back section, and order a replacement hard drive. I have purchased many drives from Alliance Peripheral Systems (APS) and have had good luck. Tell the company what kind of Mac you have, and they'll tell you what's available.

Soon, you'll get a box in the mail with a new drive that you can replace yourself with a few simple tools. Believe me, as the world's *least* handy guy (just ask my wife), this is a very easy component to install. Besides, if you get stuck, you can still take it to the shop and you'll only pay for installation.

If your hard disk is truly hosed and you can't back it up before you install a new one, call DriveSavers in Novato, California. You can send them your hard disk (or the whole computer) and they can almost always save the data for you. And they are especially nice people, as well.

**DriveSavers
800.440.1904**
www.drivesavers.com

What is a "Crash" Anyway?

When I talk about your Mac "crashing," it can mean a number of things, almost always resulting in having to restart your computer.

A crash can mean that the Mac is totally unresponsive. Your cursor is frozen on the screen, immobile. No matter what you do with the mouse or keyboard, the cursor refuses to move or to let you go back to work. This is often called being **frozen.**

Another type of crash is when the watch cursor spins for an interminable amount of time. Normally the spinning cursor means "Wait," and the Mac soon comes back to life. Unfortunately, in some instances you could wait all year and you'd still be stuck. This is commonly called being **locked up.**

A **bomb** occurs when a program has freaked out and knows it. We've all seen this dialog box:

Just to make things more complicated, people often use the terms crash, lockup, bomb, and freeze interchangeably. I do too. Just remember, anytime you hear one of these phrases it simply means your Mac has freaked out and it's time for a restart.

Crashing on Startup

It could be that sometime between when you hit the On switch and when you finally get to the Finder, your Mac is locking up. Luckily, this can be one of the easiest problems to fix: Restart the Mac with the Shift key down, which will restart without loading any of the Extensions or Control Panels. If this gets you up and running again, then you know that one of those programs needs to be removed, replaced, or reordered. On the following page are the possibilities.

You May Have an Extension Conflict

It could be that you recently installed a *new Extension or Control Panel* and it isn't getting along with one of the existing Extensions.

If you did install some new Extension or Control Panel (or maybe some other software you recently installed added something to your System Folder), see if it's something you can live without. In other words, get this troublesome little program out of your life!

If you can't remove the troublemaker because it's just too important, try to *change the order in which it loads*. Some Extensions freak out if a particular Extension has loaded before it, and some need to load after certain other ones.

Extensions/Control Panels load in alphabetical order, so typing an "A" at the beginning of the name will make it load first. The letter "Z," or even better, a tilde (~) will force an Extension to load last.

A much better way to reorder Extensions and Control Panels is to move up from Apple's Extensions Manager to a commercial program like **Now Startup** or **Conflict Catcher,** as I described in Chapter Two. Both of these utilities make it easy to specify load order and can even systematically search for which Extensions and Control Panels aren't getting along.

If you didn't just install something new and you suspect a conflict, watch your monitor at startup to see which icon appears on your screen just as the crash occurs. If you can tell which Extension is loading as the crash happens, this is probably the culprit. Turn that Extension off with an Extensions manager, or manually remove it from the System Folder.

Remember, you can tell **Now Startup** or **Conflict Catcher** to diagnose problem Extensions by automated trial-and-error restarts. It takes some time, but hey—you needed an early lunch break anyway.

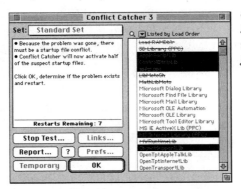

Conflict Catcher and Now Startup can run tests to see which Extensions aren't getting along.

You May Have a Corrupted Extension

If none of the above works, try replacing the offensive Extension or Control Panel with a fresh copy from a backup disk.

You May Have a Corrupted Preference File

Another item that can become corrupted is one of your Preference files. A classic example is your **Finder Preferences.** This file sits inside your Preferences folder (inside the System Folder) and is referenced by the Finder every time you startup. If this file gets damaged, you might get a crash at startup when the Finder tries to read it.

Finder Preferences

If you think this might be the problem, start your Mac from your Disk Tools or other startup disk and throw out the Finder Preferences file on your normal startup drive. Restart; the Mac will make a new Finder Preferences if it can't find one. If this doesn't help, try removing **Control Strip Preferences,** as this is another file read by some Macintoshes during startup.

You May Have a Bad Disk Driver

There is an often-ignored little piece of software that controls how your hard disk communicates with your computer called the **disk driver.**

On pages 96–97 I explained how you can use the **Drive Setup** or **HD SC Setup** program that came with your Mac to reinstall this piece of software. A bad hard disk driver can cause crashes on startup, or even random crashes after you've started successfully.

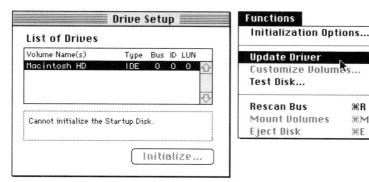

Tried everything? Still crashing? Try updating your hard disk driver with Apple HD SC Setup or Drive Setup.

Random Crashes, Bombs, and Freezes

Okay, we just spent several pages talking about crashes upon startup. But one of the most annoying Mac problems is random crashes. You're working along, everything's going fine, and boom! Either the Mac just up and freezes, or you get a System Error message.

Dozens of things can cause this type of unpredictable behavior.

Keep in mind that even the most reliable setup you can create will not make you crash-free. Since all software has bugs, you will still get some freezes, lockups, and System Errors no matter what you do.

What you want to avoid is an *unacceptable frequency* of crashes. What's unacceptable? If you use your Mac several hours a day, my rule is: **More than three crashes a week requires diagnosis and trouble-shooting.** Here are some common symptoms and fixes.

Extension Conflicts

Here we are again. Minimize the number of Extensions and Control Panels you run. If possible, specify different sets of Extensions and Control Panels for different tasks. For instance, create a set for accessing the Internet and a set for running desktop applications, then restart between tasks. Yes, you will have to restart more often, but you will crash less, and restarting is better for your computer than crashing. See Chapter Two.

Running out of RAM

Macs have a tendency to freak out when they run out of memory. Imagine you've launched a bunch of programs—so many that you've used up almost all available RAM.

Then you try to print something.

This will usually launch the program **PrintMonitor,** which runs in the background, slowly spooling the information off to the printer. Your Mac really, really, wants to run this program, but if there's not very much RAM it takes what it can, namely everything. You will crash.

If you're printing something large (say a Photoshop file), PrintMonitor may freak out because of the lack of memory and cause you to crash. Or perhaps you try to continue working in Photoshop while your Mac is printing, but your System or Finder has a nervous breakdown when it tries to access a little more memory, and then you crash.

Another RAM problem that crops up a lot has to do with the memory allocation for applications, as we discussed in Chapter Three. Most applications are allowed to launch when there is less than an optimal amount of RAM available for them. When you **Get Info** on a program, you see that the "Minimum size" of RAM allocation required is usually less than the "Preferred size." This means if an application opens and there is barely enough RAM to use it, the application will take *all* the memory that's available and there won't be any to create new pages with or to save or print with. You will crash.

Do yourself a favor. On your big applications, *set the "Minimum size" the same as the "Preferred size."* This will prevent the program from launching at all unless it has the total amount of RAM it requires to perform all of its functions.

Set the Minimum and Preferred sizes at the same amount.

Corruption

Ah yes, our insidious friend again. Try reinstalling the program you're crashing in, or at least trash its Preferences file. And read the previous sections in this chapter about all the various sorts of corruptions and what to do about it.

The Dang Thing Won't Print

Lots of things can go wrong with the printing process. Since printing consists of a long chain of sequences in which all the links must be working, it can be frustrating trying to find the one item that's causing a "break" in the chain. In addition to the inherent complexity of the situation, Apple has added several "new and improved" features and options that provide more opportunities for breakdown.

If you've been experiencing any random weirdness with printing, begin by simplifying your Macintosh's printing mechanisms. In this section we're going to deactivate some of the more troublesome printing "enhancements" that complicate things.

Naturally, if everything seems to be printing just fine—*leave it alone!* The Golden Rule of Troubleshooting is: **If it works, don't upgrade, enhance, or modify it!** Ninety percent of the problems my clients experience happen because they change things that don't need changing.

If printing has been flaky, though, the following pages suggest some good changes to make.

Nuke the PrintMonitor

As mentioned in Chapter Two, PrintMonitor sounds like a great idea: Instead of your *computer* having to send the data to be printed down the cable and into the printer, the *PrintMonitor* sends it off into RAM and your hard disk. This makes your application (Word, Excel, etc.) *think* it has printed the thing, so you get to go back to work very quickly. Meanwhile, "in the background," PrintMonitor dribbles the data down the cable and into the printer.

This can cause problems because:

- **You're "tricking" your application.** Many programs don't like being tricked.

- **PrintMonitor needs RAM that may not be available,** and generally freaks out if there isn't any.

- While the PrintMonitor is slogging away in the background, **the program you're trying to work in often becomes agonizingly slow,** defeating the whole purpose of PrintMonitor.

- It's one more *unnecessary link* in the chain.

To turn PrintMonitor off:

- Go to the Apple Menu and select "Chooser."
- Click the "Off" button below "Background Printing." If you don't see Background Printing listed, don't worry about it, it's already off.

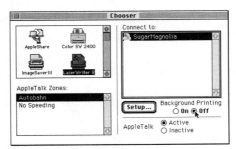

*Turning PrintMonitor off can solve many printing problems. I **always** leave it off.*

Kill QuickDraw GX

With System 7.5, Apple introduced a whole new-and-improved set of optional software for printing called **QuickDraw GX.** The problem with this software is that hardly any software developers updated their programs to take advantage of the cool new features that QuickDraw GX made available.

In addition, QuickDraw GX takes up a lot more RAM than standard printing software, and it can make some applications more prone to printing problems.

The good news is that you probably are not using QuickDraw GX anyway, as it does not get installed on your Mac unless you've consciously installed it yourself.

If you previously installed QuickDraw GX and now want to remove it, **turn off the GX Extensions** using Extensions Manager, as outlined in Chapter Two. Or use the same software that installed GX to remove it: pop in your install disk, double-click the installer icon, and choose the cool "Custom Remove" option.

Many installers have a "remove" option as well as an "install" option.

Make the Right Laser Printer Connection

It's important that your computer and your printer are talking to each other. That means not only having a cable between them, but the *right kind* of cable and the proper driver software. If you are using just one Mac and one printer, all you need is the simple serial cable between the two, which is probably what you already have and it works just fine.

If you have two Macs (or more) that you want to connect to the same printer, you need an **AppleTalk** connection. AppleTalk is a networking protocol that allows two or more devices to communicate back and forth. Generally, you have to have special **LocalTalk Connector** boxes plugged into all your devices for this to work. These special connector boxes run about 10 bucks and look like this:

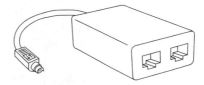

1. Plug this gadget into your Mac's printer or modem port (yup, the modem port works great for printing; you can also connect your modem to the printer port). Plug another connector into the printer, connect the two, and you're set.

2. The next step is to jump into the **Network Control Panel** and make sure it knows what's going on. Open the Network Control Panel and choose **LocalTalk Built In.**

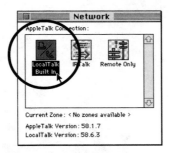

3. Turn the printer on.

4. After the printer is warmed up, open the **Chooser** from the Apple Menu. In the Chooser, first make sure that AppleTalk is Active.

5. On the left side of the window, the Chooser displays the **printer drivers** that are available. Click on the type that most closely represents the printer you're printing to, and on the right side you should see the device itself listed. Click on it. Close the Chooser.

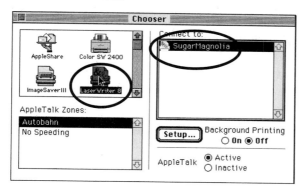

6. You should now be able to print.

Make the Right StyleWriter Connection

To connect to a device that does not have any AppleTalk networking capabilities, such as the Apple StyleWriter or ImageWriter, go to the **Chooser** and make sure that **AppleTalk is Inactive.** On the left side of the dialog box, choose the appropriate driver, and on the right choose whether the printer is connected to the printer or the modem port.

That's it—the software and hardware should now be in synch to print correctly.

The Mac Says There's No Printer

Let's say you've made AppleTalk active in the Chooser, picked the correct driver, and the printer name fails to appear on the right. That could mean one of several things:

- **The printer is turned off.** Turn the printer on, wait a minute or so for it to warm up, and try again.

- **The printer isn't warmed up enough.** If you go to the Chooser before the printer has gone through its warm-up exercises, the Chooser won't see it. Close the Chooser and don't open it again until you are sure the printer has finished its business and is ready to get to work.

- **There's a loose connection.** Make sure all the cables are firmly plugged in on all ends.

- **Your printer isn't a LocalTalk device.** A few laser printers, like the Apple Personal LaserWriter 300, use inexpensive QuickDraw technology instead of PostScript to convert your documents into little dots on paper. These printers usually also lack networking capabilities. In that case, you connect to the printer using the same method as you do for a Style-Writer or ImageWriter (page 127).

  Most laser printers have expensive PostScript brains inside that print better and faster and are able to be networked.

- **A component has freaked out.** Either your Mac or your printer could have had a minor nervous breakdown. Turn them both off, restart them, and try again.

The Mac Sees the Printer, but Still Won't Print

What if you're all connected, the computer "sees" the printer, and yet the dang pages won't come out?

- **Make sure PrintMonitor is off.** As mentioned before, this program can often cause problems. This is one of them.

- **Print fewer pages at a time.** For whatever reason—too many fonts, too many pages, or too large/complex images— you can often bypass this problem by printing fewer pages, perhaps even one at a time.

- **If you're using TrueType on a PostScript printer, change the font.** As detailed in Chapter Ten, PostScript printers don't like TrueType fonts.

- **Take a break.** Some software or hardware may have freaked out. Save, quit, turn off the hardware, restart, and try again.

- **Change things**. Some application could have messed up. Maybe the graphic you created in FreeHand has some weird bug in it. Maybe the printer driver has a mistake in the code. Maybe the printer's ROMs are batty. Perhaps a font is corrupt. Try a different font, replace some of the graphics, go back to an earlier version of the document. Just mess around, make changes, and often things will work again.

Important Things to Remember

- Make frequent backups.
- Don't change or update your hardware or software unless you have to.
- Perform the important rituals described in Chapter Five.
- Make sure you have Disk First Aid and Norton Utilities, and use them before doing anything drastic like reformatting your hard disk.
- Reinstall your System Folder from scratch for a fast fix to many problems.
- If your hard disk goes bad, get a new one from mail order and install it yourself.
- Use an Extensions manager and turn off unnecessary items.
- Keep your documents simple for easy printing.

Invaluable Accessories 7

What? More Stuff for the System Folder?

A running theme throughout this book has been to minimize, minimize, minimize, especially when it comes to Extensions and Control Panels. In this chapter I recommend doing the opposite—I encourage you to install additional software that will bloat your System Folder even further!

Why the flip-flop? Simple. The software discussed here will make your life so much easier that any additional RAM-gobbling and crash-causing will be worth it.

Of course you should have already done a survey of your System Folder with the Extensions Manager and turned off all unnecessary Extensions and Control Panels. With that done, adding a few of these little gems should cause few or no problems.

These are utilities the pros use everyday and all the time. They will streamline almost every operation and allow you to maximize your Mac's potential to the point where your computer can be doing work for you—even when you're not around!

The three programs listed are by no means the only add-ons I recommend. These are the ones that I *insist* on having installed on my Mac at all times. Here they are in order of priority.

Now Super Boomerang

Super Boomerang

Wouldn't it be great if you could open and find needed documents almost instantly without having to go to the Finder and wade through the Find command? Imagine doing a "Save As" and navigating to the required folder using a simple keyboard shortcut—no more clicking the Desktop button and burrowing down to the desired location. Super Boomerang can do this kind of stuff and more.

Super Boomerang is part of the popular Now Utilities software package ($85, mail order), which contains a dozen programs of varying degrees of usefulness. Many folks install the whole batch of them. My advice is to install the Super Boomerang portion only, get to know it, and then evaluate the rest of them to possibly install later.

The Installer will put a Control Panel in your System Folder that modifies how Open and Save dialog boxes operate.

The most obvious change is that at the top of an Open or Save dialog box a menu bar appears:

Super Boomerang adds a very powerful menu to the top of your Open or Save dialog boxes.

The Folder menu in Super Boomerang contains a list of recently accessed folders; choose one to "jump" to that folder instantly. From the File menu, you can immediately open recently used files. Naturally, the Drive menu does the same for mounted volumes.

You can type a keystroke combination while choosing a folder or file from the Folder, File, or Drive menu, then that combination becomes the standard keyboard shortcut for that file, folder, or drive. This means the next time you Open or Save As, you just type the shortcut to access that folder or open that file!

One of the easiest features to use in Super Boomerang is its ability to remember recently accessed folders.

The Preferences command under the Options menu allows you to set a variety of options, including the choice of making a folder or file permanent, which keeps it on the list forever.

Another great benefit of this program is that a new submenu appears under the Open command in all applications. It lists all recently edited files, which makes opening files even faster.

The best feature of all is also one of the lesser-used ones—finding files. Imagine I wrote a letter a few months ago to an associate (let's say his name's Fred), and I need to review it. Easy. Assuming I'm in my word processing program, these are the steps:

1. From the File menu, choose "Open...."

2. Type Command F (or choose "Find..." from the Super Boomerang Option menu).

3. In the Find dialog box, type "fred" and hit Return (I'm assuming I used the word "Fred" in the file name).

4. The Find dialog box will return a list of files with "fred" in the name (it only finds files that the application you're in will open). Double-click the file you want, and you're in business!

Since the Find feature works in context of the application you're working in, it would ignore spreadsheets or graphics that had "fred" in the name. This makes the search much more useful than a generic name search in the Finder, which returns a list of *everything* that has a name match.

In any Open dialog box, you can type Command F to find files that you want to open— much more convenient than Apple's Find File feature.

What if you can't remember the name? Super Boomerang will search for the contents of a file as well (although it takes longer). All you have to do is enter your search string in the "Scan for" area, and let it go! Not only will Boomerang find files that contain the search string, but it will let you see how many times the string is used in the document *and* show you the contents of the file without having to open it!

It's funny—one of the main reasons I fight using Windows machines on an everyday basis is not because of ease-of-use or user interface issues. It's because there is no equivalent program to Super Boomerang on that platform! Do yourself a big favor and get to know this ultra-useful program.

QuicKeys

QuicKeys

Remember the promise of the personal computer? It was designed to be a labor-saving device that would make all of our lives easier. It would automate mundane office tasks so we could do more interesting things with our lives. One problem is that most people are still doing the same old things every day, over and over—except they now use a computer to do them!

But power users let their computers work harder and smarter by automating tasks with macros and scripts. Imagine creating a list of tasks in a language your Mac or even individual applications can understand, then assigning each task a keyboard shortcut, or even a clickable icon. Not only can this save you from the effort of doing all the steps of the task yourself, but it can save time dramatically.

For instance, here's a set of steps I do several times a day: I tell my Mac to open the Chooser, I choose a certain zone on the network, pick a particular printer, and close the Chooser. Doing it manually takes about 13 seconds. Since I turned it into a macro, it only takes 2 seconds, and I never even touch the mouse! I've seen tasks that would take a human hours to do, turned into a single command that is performed automatically while the user goes on a coffee break!

You have a bunch of different ways to do this kind of thing. They range from complex programming to simple record-and-playback programs. Most experts agree the best combination of ease and power is the program **QuicKeys.**

When you install QuicKeys, you get an Extension and a Control Panel that work together. These allow you to create macros for any application (including the System and Finder) and can even create "universal" macros that work with all applications.

It's awesome! QuicKeys can record things you do and even let you edit the individual steps.

At its most basic level, you can ask QuicKeys to lurk in the background, watch what you do, and record a list of the steps involved. Then you can stop the recording and assign it a keyboard shortcut or icon. This simple type of macro can be enough to simplify life greatly. Here's an example:

> For years, launching applications required burrowing into your hard disk and opening folders to find application icons to double-click on. System 7 made this easier with the introduction of aliases, but gee—shouldn't you be able to use a simple keyboard shortcut to launch a program? It takes just a few seconds to define a shortcut using QuicKeys:

1. Go to the QuicKeys Menu and choose "QuicKeys...."

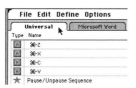

2. In the main QuicKeys Editor, choose the "Universal" tab. This will permit the macro to run no matter which program you're in.

3. Go to the Define menu and choose "File Launch...."

4. Navigate through the dialog box and double-click on the file or application you want to open.

5. Assign a keyboard shortcut in the "File Launch" dialog box: just type the key combination you want to use and QuicKeys will record it.

6. Click "OK" to exit QuicKeys.

Congratulations! You can now start up or switch to the chosen application without so much as picking up the mouse.

Here's another example of a QuicKey shortcut I programmed (actually, it's the first shortcut I ever made): A few years ago I noticed that Microsoft applications enabled you to use the Escape key on the keyboard to "click" the Cancel button in dialog boxes. Most of my other programs didn't allow this, so I used QuicKeys to force those programs to do the same. Now most programs allow you to use the Escape key to Cancel, but you can adapt these steps to the shortcut of your choice.

1. Go to the QuicKeys menu and choose "QuicKeys...."

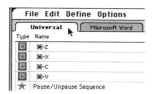

2. In the main QuicKeys Editor, click the "Universal" tab.

3. Go to the Define menu and choose "Buttons…."

4. In the "Name" area of the dialog box, type the word "Cancel."

Select the "Keystroke" area, then hit the Escape key on your keyboard. QuicKeys will record the stroke.

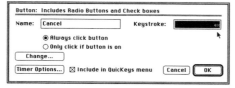

5. Click "OK" to exit QuicKeys.

You can assign shortcuts to buttons, menu commands, practically anything! Wouldn't it be great if all your programs had the same keyboard shortcuts for the same commands? With QuicKeys, you can make this happen in just a few minutes.

QuicKeys can also record long, complex sequences. The AppleScript Extension from Apple can do even more; however, it's also much more difficult to program.

RAM Doubler

RAM Doubler

RAM Doubler is one of those things that sounds too good to be true. Install a piece of software, restart your Mac, and suddenly your computer thinks it has twice or even three times as much memory? Can't work, can it?

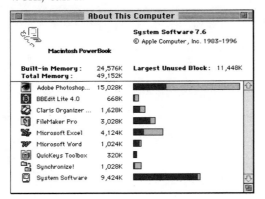

RAM Doubler has tricked this Mac into thinking it has twice as much memory as what is built in.

This program does some amazing tricks to fool your Mac into thinking it has more RAM than is actually installed. This is what it does:

- It compresses the background applications (the ones you are not actively using) in memory to take up less space. This makes more memory available for the active application.

- If not enough memory can be reclaimed through this technique to simulate double the physical RAM, some of the background items may be temporarily off-loaded to disk as virtual memory.

What does all this do for you? It lets you run more programs at the same time. It does *not* let you give one application a ton more RAM than you normally would. Don't fall into the trap some Photoshop users have, where they buy an 8-megabyte machine, install RAM Doubler, and think they now have 13 or so megabytes for image editing. Do that kind of thing and you're headed for Crashville, USA.

The tricks that RAM Doubler pulls can slow your machine down a teeny bit, particularly as you switch from one program to another, but this is more than made up for by the time saved from not having to launch and quit programs so often.

Will you have more crashes and lockups? Yup. Of course! It's an Extension! I have heard some complain that they've had to remove RAM Doubler because of the problems it's caused. This happens a lot to people who have just bought a brand-new Macintosh. RAM Doubler needs to be updated to run on the latest and greatest Macintosh—make sure you get the very most recent version of the software, especially if you use Photoshop. Sometimes something will conflict with RAM Doubler (maybe a screen saver, a sound-making Extension, or another piece of frivolous software). Sometimes the user allocates too much RAM to one program. Personally, I've been using it for years, and it's been practically bulletproof.

Important Things to Remember

- Super Boomerang is the best part of the Now Utilities package. It makes your Open and Save dialog boxes much easier to use and way more powerful.

- QuicKeys lets you record your own keyboard shortcuts for menu commands, dialog box buttons, and even long sequences of commands and procedures.

- RAM Doubler is a great way to run several programs at the same time.

Manage Text Right

Don't Let Your Text Control You!

I've watched thousands of people learn and use the most popular software programs, and what's really amazing is that *very few people use their applications the way they were designed to be used.*

I mean, if the programmers who write these applications watched the average person use their creation, they'd be astounded. Microsoft actually did this several years ago. They observed experienced Microsoft Word users at work. They were floored. It turned out that fewer than one out of five people were using Microsoft Word's most basic features the way the programmers had envisioned.

A classic example of this is the way millions of people use their word processing programs. **Most don't ever set tab stops.** The vast majority hit the Spacebar fifty times in a row to "push" something into position. A programmer would say, "Geez, all they have to do is use that easy Ruler feature I designed, and they could quickly move that text just about wherever they wanted—it would sure be a lot faster than what they're doing now!"

It's really a vicious circle—people are working way too hard and taking too long to do things. As a consequence, they don't have time to learn how to use their software correctly. Let's look at the whys and wherefores and what to do about it.

So Why is There a Problem

There are three causes for this not-using-the-features-right problem.

1. Most people buy the wrong program.

I call this the "macho" approach to buying software. When people are deciding what software to buy, they often default to the one with the *most features*. I've heard it a million times, "I bought Product X because it's the most powerful." The problem is: **the more features a program has, the more difficult it is to keep it simple and easy to understand.**

This penchant for features almost killed PageMaker a few years back. The folks at Aldus (it used to be Aldus PageMaker—Adobe bought Aldus in 1994, so now it's Adobe PageMaker) looked at 85 percent of their market and discovered it was the secretary/businessperson producing the company newsletter. Aldus designed a simple, easy, almost-perfect product for them. They figured they'd lose some of their super high-end users to a much more confusing product— QuarkXPress, but hey, that 85 percent they'd still have locked up!

They were dead wrong.

When people read the magazine reviews (actually nobody reads the reviews, they just turn to the last page where the features are listed on the left, and each program gets a column where bullets indicate which features the program has), they said, "Dang! Quark has more features! That's the one for me!"

Also when the newsletter people (85 percent) started talking to the hotshot designer people (15 percent), the design types would look down their bolo ties and say something like, "Oh, you use PageMaker— how quaint." The poor PageMaker users no longer felt macho, and man, people couldn't dump PageMaker fast enough.

To be fair, PageMaker did have some glaring deficiencies that Aldus simply refused to fix, and all along Quark was improving the usability of XPress.

Adobe is now playing the game right, and today PageMaker actually surpasses QuarkXPress in many key areas. The target audience of users generally doesn't even begin to scratch the surface of the power available in that program.

2. Most software is cryptic

Software companies—even ones who try hard—have a terrible time making programs that are easy to master. Software engineers have a tough time relating to how the rest of the world thinks and often implement features in a counter-intuitive way.

Even though Microsoft has spent millions trying to make their software more usable, the result is a confusing plethora of buttons and "Wizards." Microsoft says, "Gee, people sure have problems understanding how to do (insert command or sequence here); rather than just make it easier to understand, let's make a button do it!" Another Microsoft approach is to use a Wizard. A Wizard pops up when you click a button, and a series of dialog boxes interrogates you endlessly as to what you are attempting.

Claris FileMaker is a great example of one of the few programs that does a good job of combining power and ease-of-use: it doesn't have the greatest number of features, but it has more than most database programs, and it's easy to learn and use.

3. Nobody reads the manuals

It's too bad really. Ten years ago software manuals generally stunk, and ever since that time they've had a bad rap. I recently told a client where in their manual they could find some information they were looking for, and they said, "The manual's lousy, I never touch it." In fact, the manual had recently won some awards for being so complete and easy to follow! This person had probably given up on manuals a long time ago and had never even picked up this one.

That's not to say that there aren't some imperfect manuals out there—a significant number of poor manuals are still being written. While ten years ago manuals were big and incomprehensible, today the problem is reversed. Many manuals today are **small, well written, and incomplete.** The nice thing about today's manuals is that you can sit down and read through them quickly. The problem is that the features are skimmed over lightly, without much detail or context.

Another problem with manuals is that they are designed as a reference—they try to list program features and what they do. They're more like a dictionary really. What's missing is a prioritization of what's really important and what's not. Manuals are also light on describing procedures to complete a task.

While most manuals are not perfect, you should still read them. At the very least, you'll pick up the correct terms for features in your software. This means later on you can look them up in the index for a reminder of how they work.

The Essentials

Almost everybody uses a **word processor** of some kind. Most use either Microsoft Word 6.0 or ClarisWorks 4.0. I'll be using those two programs as examples in this chapter. It doesn't really matter what program you use because all of the major word processors have the features described below. Knowing these features moves you into true "Power User" status.

I've spent years watching the experts use all the popular word processors, and I have some solid recommendations for what features and shortcuts you should focus on.

Even if you use high-end desktop publishing programs like Adobe PageMaker or QuarkXPress to format your text files, these are the text handling features you really must take advantage of. Although I'm focusing on Word and ClarisWorks, every feature mentioned here also applies to PageMaker and XPress.

Paragraph Formatting vs. Character Formatting

Okay, so you know how to highlight text and make it bold or change its font, right? What about when you want to **center a heading?** You may be thinking, "Well, I just highlight the entire heading and then apply the centering command . . . right?"

Wrong. You do *not* have to highlight anything. All you need is the blinking cursor (called the insertion point) in the text. Notice in the example below that nothing is highlighted, but it centers anyway!

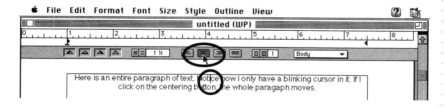

Here's the deal: Alignment, indents, tab stops, spacing, and most other attributes that control the *location* of text apply to the *entire paragraph in which the cursor is located.* This is called **paragraph formatting.** Try it: click in some text, then click on the Center Alignment button in your Ruler.

A Word about Word
Many Mac users have the most recent version of Word, version 6.0, which is why I am using it as an example in this book. In real life, I avoid it like the plague. Word 6.0 is generally regarded among Mac experts as being significantly more confusing and slower than the previous version. Every technique described in this chapter is made easier if you go back to the 5.1 version of Word.

Well then, what's a paragraph?

What do I mean by a "paragraph"? You create a paragraph *every time you hit the Return key*. If you have a return address that is three lines long and you hit a Return after each line, you have three paragraphs. Every word processing and page layout program works this way.

So, what if you need to center *two* paragraphs? Naturally, you would have to highlight if you wanted to center more than one paragraph.

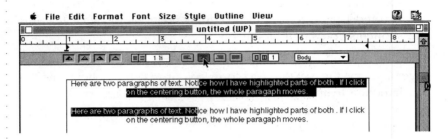

Even though neither paragraph in the example above is highlighted entirely, the centering command works great. Highlighting a little text in each paragraph is like having a blinking cursor in each paragraph.

Character formatting

So, why does it require highlighting to change a *font?* Ah! Font, size, and attribute changes (like bold and italic) are **character formatting**. When you do that kind of thing, you are changing the size and shape *of individual letters*. You must highlight the text because your word processor needs to know *which* individual characters are going to be changed.

The bottom line:

If you're changing the *location* of the text, it's **paragraph formatting**.

If you're changing the way letters *look,* it's **character formatting**.

Type first and format later!

Expert document creators save themselves tons of time by typing their entire document first and worrying about the paragraph formatting later. Thanks to the **Styles** feature, along with Word's Repeat command (both described in this chapter), you can format vast quantities of text in short order.

Setting Indents: The Ruler Rules

How do you get text to be indented, that is, pushed over to the right?

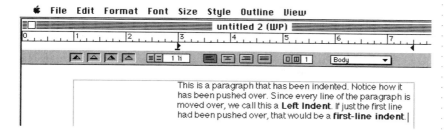

Indent with the Ruler, not the Spacebar or Tab key

If you typically indent with the Tab key (or, heaven forbid, the Space-bar), you must read this section because you've been working way too hard! Here's the easy way to do it:

- Put your **cursor in the paragraph** you want to push over.
- Drag the **indent markers** that are on the left side of the Ruler over to the right.

Huh? The indent markers? What are they?

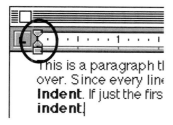

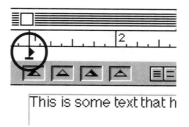

In Word, the indent markers look like little triangles facing each other, with a box underneath.

In ClarisWorks, the indent markers look like a black triangle and a horizontal bar underneath.

If you drag **both markers** over to the right together, the entire selected paragraph becomes left-indented.

To do this in Word 6 (shown below), drag that **little box** at the bottom and both markers move in tandem.

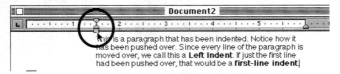

In ClarisWorks (shown below), carefully position the very tip of the pointer on just the **black triangle marker** and drag. Both the triangle and the horizontal bar marker at the bottom will move together.

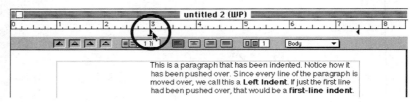

An important point: Even though it looks like there is only one Ruler at the top of your screen, there could really be thousands! *Every paragraph has its very own Ruler.* Every time you hit the Return key you make a new Ruler. Your software only shows you the one your cursor is sitting in. If you highlight more than one paragraph, it tries to show you one Ruler that represents several paragraphs.

Creating first-line indents is just as easy as making left indents. First, of course, highlight the paragraphs you want to indent.

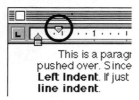

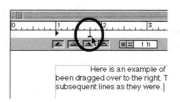

*In Word, drag **just** the top indent marker triangle to the right.*

*In ClarisWorks, drag **just** the horizontal bar indent marker that sits underneath the triangle to the right.*

Setting Tabs: The Return of the Ruler

Everybody creates tables. Almost all word processors these days include complex table-making commands and features. Most folks should just use their Old Friend the Ruler to produce tabular material —it's easy!

What if you needed to make a table like this:

Item	Price
Pez Dispenser	$2.95
LickemAid	$0.55
SweeTarts	$0.85
Fizzies	$0.99

What's the easiest way to create this table? Here's what to do:

- Type the word "Item" and hit the Tab key once. *Your cursor won't move very far. That's okay.* Type the word "Price" and hit the Return key.

- Type "Pez Dispenser" and hit tab once. Type "$2.95" and hit Return.

- **Repeat this sequence** until you have typed the entire table. Do not hit any extra Tabs!

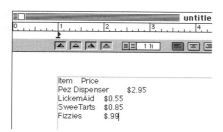

Hmmm . . . things may not be lining up the way you want them. That's okay, because *your word processor thinks they line up beautifully!* To the program, the **structure** is perfect.

The problem is that the **tab stops** on the Ruler(s) need to be adjusted. Here's what's happening: Most word processors set up default tab stops every half-inch or so, even if you can't see them. That means every time you hit the Tab key *the cursor jumps to line up with the next tab stop.* At most, your cursor will move a half-inch.

What you need to do is tell the Ruler to get rid of those silly standard tab stops and put in your own instead. In this case you have five paragraphs (you hit Return five times) and five Rulers to adjust.

In **Claris Works:**

If you want the column to line up on the left, use a **left-aligned** tab marker.

If you want the column to line up on the right, use a **right-aligned** tab marker.

If you want the column to line up centered, use a **center-aligned** tab marker.

If you want the column to line up on the periods in the numbers, use a **decimal-aligned** tab marker.

■ Highlight the paragraphs that need adjustment.

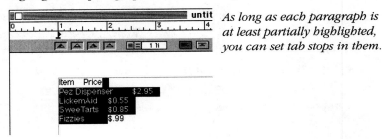

As long as each paragraph is at least partially highlighted, you can set tab stops in them.

■ Next, **drag a tab stop** onto the Ruler (which will actually put it onto all **five** Rulers because all five paragraphs are selected): drag one of the four tab icons (they look like little pyramids) onto the Ruler. Once the tab is set, the numbers line up! *And all the tabs to the left of your own tab will disappear.* This is important to know.

■ If you want the column to **line up on the right,** use a right-aligned tab stop: press-and-drag the third tab marker up to the Ruler to set a right-aligned tab stop.

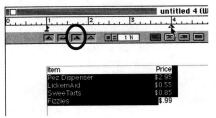

The third tab icon in the row of markers is the right-aligned tab. You can tell because the dark side of the pyramid is a clue that the text will align on that side.

If you decide to **get rid of a tab stop** in either Word or Works, just press-and-drag the marker down off the Ruler.

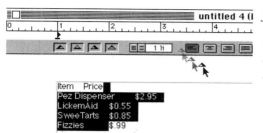

Just press-and-drag a tab marker off the Ruler to get rid of it. You can let go once your pointer has left the Ruler.

In **Microsoft Word 6.0,** you do essentially the same thing as I just explained for ClarisWorks, with some minor variations.

First, type the table, and highlight it as described above. Then go to the left edge of the Ruler and choose a tab stop by clicking on the **Tab Alignment Button.** Each time you click, another type of tab marker will appear.

After you highlight the text, click on the Tab Alignment Button until the correct tab marker appears.

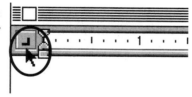

Click on the Tab Alignment Button to choose a type of tab stop:

This is the **left-aligned** tab marker.

This is the **right-aligned** tab marker.

This is the **center-aligned** tab marker.

This is the **decimal-aligned** tab marker.

Shown below are the tab markers in Word 5.1. From left to right they are left-aligned, centered, right-aligned, and decimal. Just click on the one you want to use, then click in the Ruler.

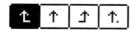

Next, **click in the Ruler** where you want the tab stop to be positioned.

After choosing a tab marker, just click in the Ruler to position it.

To get rid of a tab stop, drag it down and off the Ruler.

Viewing Invisible Characters

When you're the one doing the typing, it's easy to know when you've hit the Tab, Spacebar, or Return key. What about if somebody else typed the document and you have to format it? Being able to see exactly how someone constructed things can be a real timesaver.

Luckily, all word processors (as well as PageMaker and XPress) can show you these normally invisible characters.

 In **Word,** click the **Show/Hide ¶** button.

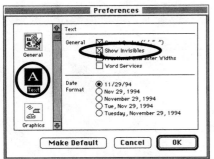

In **ClarisWorks,** from the Edit Menu, choose "Preferences...."

Click the Text icon on the left.

Click "Show Invisibles."

Click OK.

Now you can see where Spaces, Tabs, and Returns were typed:

Hidden characters revealed!

Spacing: Watch Your Return Policy

Another common formatting faux pas is the ol' Double-Return Scenario. Hey—you want space between your paragraphs, right?

The problem with hitting double Returns is that it creates huge, unsightly gaps between paragraphs. And on documents longer than one page, you can end up with the margins looking funny. If a new page or column begins right where you've hit two Returns, the page or column starts one line too low! This looks unprofessional:

WELCOME TO CLARISWORKS 4.0!
Thank you for choosing the ClarisWorks® 4.0 product. We're excited about this latest release of ClarisWorks and know that it will help you to be more productive and creative. This Read Me file documents some additional tips that may prove helpful when using ClarisWorks 4.0, including changes for users of previous versions of the program. In particular, this document provides information about:

I. New features in ClarisWorks 4.0

USABILITY AND DESIGN CHANGES IN VERSION 4.0
Editing Charts and Formatting Chart Elements
In previous versions of ClarisWorks, chart elements such as axes labels and legend text took their font, size and size attributes from the formatting of the cells being charted in the ClarisWorks spreadsheet. If the formatting changed, so did the chart.

Sure, you could go through the document and fix the margin problems one-by-one by adding and removing Returns, but what if you edit the text later? Everything reflows and you must go back in and redo it all! And you would still have unsightly gaps between paragraphs.

There's a much better way to solve all these problems. It's called **paragraph spacing.** Both Word and ClarisWorks (as well as PageMaker and XPress) have commands under the Format menu called "Paragraph." This command brings up a dialog box that lets you adjust the space between paragraphs.

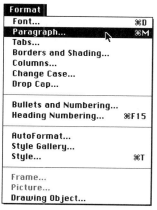

For all your spacing needs, choose the "Paragraph…" command from the Format menu.

In PageMaker you'll find this command under the Type menu. In XPress, choose "Formats…" from the Style menu.

Here's a good way to set things up.

In ClarisWorks: Create a new document. From the Format menu, choose "Paragraph…," then enter "1" line in the "Space Before" box. Or you could press on the little menu that now says "li" and choose another measure, such as points, and enter a value.

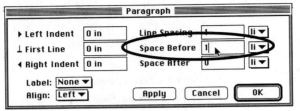

You can specify how many lines of space between paragraphs, or how many points, millimeters, etc.

In Word: Go into the **Spacing** area of the **Paragraph** dialog box and type 12 points in the **Before** text box (12 points is roughly the same as one line).

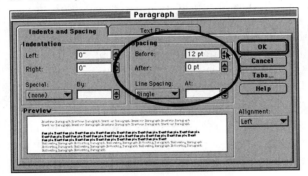

Word lets you specify the number of points of space between paragraphs.

You can just as easily use **Spacing After** instead of Spacing Before to get the same effect. For some reason, most people prefer to use Spacing Before instead. *(I never use Spacing Before in paragraphs because then I get awkward spaces when a head or subhead is followed by a paragraph. I always use Spacing After in paragraphs, and Spacing Before in heads and subheads. —Robin)*

Now—when you type some text and hit Return, you'll automatically get a nice space between each paragraph. The cool part is that the gap will intelligently vanish when a paragraph falls at the top of a page or column. It will then magically reappear should you edit and the text moves out of that position.

In the description of **Styles** that follows, the benefits of this spacing stuff becomes even more apparent.

Paragraph Styles: The Biggest Timesaver

For most people (including you, whether or not you know it yet), how to create paragraph styles is the most important feature to understand in a word processor or page layout program. **Styles,** (or **style sheets,** as they're sometimes called) allow you to define, or record, the formatting of a paragraph and apply that formatting to other unformatted text. The bottom line: instant and consistent formatting.

It gets even better. After you've formatted an entire document, you can make global formatting changes almost instantly.

Let's say you've got a fifty-page report, and the boss wants all the headings a "little bigger." If you've used a style sheet, it takes ten seconds to reformat all of them.

Both Word and ClarisWorks have two kinds of styles: **character and paragraph.** PageMaker and XPress have paragraph styles, not character styles.

> **Paragraph styles** allow you to format an entire paragraph all at once with nothing more than a blinking cursor inside the selected paragraph. The downside is that you cannot style just one word inside a paragraph—if you try, the entire paragraph reformats.

> **Character styles** require that you highlight the text you want to format, but they do not allow you to define formatting such as alignment, tabs, or spacing (do those in paragraph styles).

As a general rule, paragraph styles are more powerful and useful than character styles, which is why I focus on them in this chapter.

The following pages describe how to tackle that fifty-page report.

Defining a Style in Word 6.0

Let's say you've spent a few minutes getting a heading to look just right, and you know you're going to be using this format several times throughout the document.

In Word 6, to create a Style out of the heading all you do is:

- Make sure your **cursor is inside** the heading.
- Click in the **Style Box** in the Toolbar—it should highlight the inside of the box.
- Type in a descriptive name such as "Heading" and hit the Return key. Word will record the name and its formatting.

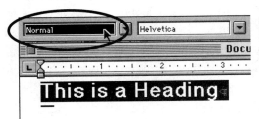

Click in the Style box to type a name to define a style.

Be careful though, because Word 6 has already reserved a ton (76 to be exact) of Style names for its own internal use. If you try to use the name "Title" for example, Word will not define a new Style for you—instead, it will assume you want to use the predefined "Title" Style, and (argh!) your text will reformat.

Word 6 will *not* allow you to delete or effectively rename these pre-made styles. Word 5.1 on the other hand, lets you do both of these things.

To get around this Word 6 limitation, I often put an "@" at the beginning of my style names. For example, if I wanted to call something **Heading 1** (an "illegal" name—Word 6 has already reserved it), I would call it **@Heading 1.** Another benefit of putting an @ at the beginning of the name is that Word puts *your* Styles (vs. the ones Word has predefined) at the top of the Styles list.

Defining a Style in ClarisWorks

As in Word, begin by formatting a paragraph to make it look the way you want it. Then:

- Make sure you have the cursor inside the formatted text.
- From the View menu, choose "Show Styles."

 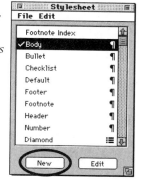

The "Show Styles" command in the View menu brings up the Stylesheet palette.

- Click the **New** button on the Stylesheet palette.

- **Type a name** for the Style.
  Make it a **Paragraph** Style.
  Base it on **None.**
  Put a check in **Inherit document selection format.**

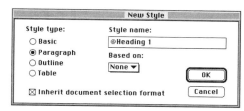

After you click the New button on the Stylesheet palette, you can name a new Style in this dialog box.

Basing the Style on "None" means the Style will not make any of its formatting decisions based on what happens to other Styles. Checking the box "Inherit document selection format" is crucial; you're telling ClarisWorks to define the Style based on the formatting used in the paragraph where your cursor is currently located.

- Finally, with your cursor still in the same paragraph, **click in the palette on the Style name you just defined.** This will tell the paragraph you used as an example to assume that Style.

Applying Styles in Both Word and ClarisWorks

Now comes the fun part. You can quickly go through the document and "tag" all the other headings to assume the same format.

Both Word and ClarisWorks have **Style menus** in their Rulers/Toolbars:

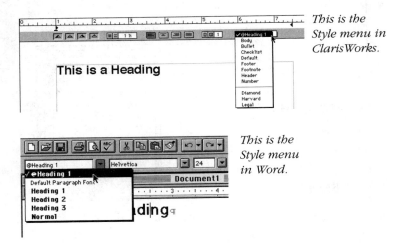

This is the Style menu in ClarisWorks.

This is the Style menu in Word.

All you have to do is click in one of the paragraphs (or select several paragraphs in a row) that you want to become the @Heading1 Style, then choose that Style from the menu. The paragraph will **automatically reformat.**

> A very cool keyboard shortcut (in Word only) is **Command Y.** Command Y is the shortcut for "do that again." If you clicked in some text and chose a Style from the menu, you can immediately click in another paragraph and use Command Y to apply the same Style without having to go up to the Toolbar!

Okay, what if you go ahead and format the entire document—and then you need to make the headings look different? This is where the power of Styles really shows its stuff. Modifying Styles is easy.

Modifying Styles in Word 6.0

Let's say you want to make all the headings a little smaller. All you have to do is:

- Highlight any one of the headings and reformat it.

- Go back to the Style menu on the Toolbar, and choose the same Style name (as the one you're already using) again.

- This confuses Word a bit and it will ask if you want to **Redefine** or **Restyle** @Heading1. Choose Redefine, and all the headings that have @Heading1 Style applied will automatically change!

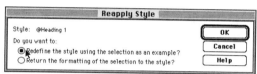

If you try to re-tag a style to a paragraph that already has a Style tag, you'll get this dialog box.

Modifying Styles in ClarisWorks

You can do the same thing in ClarisWorks:

- **Click** in one of the headings.

- Bring up the **Style Sheet palette.** You may have to go to the View menu to bring it up.

- The Style you want to edit will be **highlighted** in the palette, since you've clicked in a paragraph that has that Style.

Change a highlighted style by clicking the Edit button.

- **Click the Edit button** at the bottom of the palette. The palette will expand to show the Style's properties and your cursor will change into an odd-looking "S."

- **Go into the menus or the Ruler** and make changes to the @Heading1 Style. When you're finished, **all** the paragraphs that have been "tagged" as @Heading1 will change!

This funny-looking cursor tells you that making changes to text formatting will affect all the paragraphs with the selected style.

Important Things to Remember

- To change any paragraph formatting, you can select the entire paragraph simply by having a cursor anywhere inside the paragraph.

- Alignment, tabs, and indents are all paragraph formats.

- Character formatting requires that you highlight all the characters you want to change. Character formatting affects the shapes and sizes of the letters.

- Font, size, attribute (bold, italic, etc.) are all character formats.

- Setting tab stops on the Ruler is much better than using the Spacebar or multiple default Tabs to move type into position.

- View the invisible characters to see what is going on with your text.

- Use Paragraph Spacing controls instead of multiple Returns.

- Use Paragraph Styles (style sheets) to quickly format and reformat text. (And remember to include paragraph spacing controls in your style sheets.)

Get Great Graphics

9

Making it Look Good

Graphics and publishing—odds are that if you're reading this book, you're either creating graphics and publishing pages already, or you will be soon.

The Macintosh is the computer of choice for ninety percent of the graphics professionals worldwide. Even amateurs now have access to computer-based publishing equipment and software that just a few years ago would have cost tens of thousands of dollars.

I have had the privilege of working closely with some of the world's top Mac publishing experts over the years. Here are the most useful concepts I've learned and techniques I've picked up.

Imaging Essentials

Many people get lost when trying to understand the various types of graphics that can be created on the Mac. It's easy to see why. You've got dozens of programs to choose from, such as Illustrator, Free-Hand, Canvas, Photoshop, Painter, Sketcher, and more. These programs can create files in all kinds of formats, including TIFF, EPS, PICT, PNT, GIF, and JPEG.

It can be difficult to clearly understand which program should be used to create which format and how they all differ.

Let's make it easy. First of all, you should know that graphics created by or for the Mac will fall neatly into one of two categories.

They are either:

- Graphics made of little colored tiles, like dots, or . . .
- Graphics made of mathematical descriptions, as shapes.

An Image as Dots

Way back in 1984 when the Macintosh was introduced, it came with a cute little program called **MacPaint.** MacPaint was a trendsetter. It was the first computer program with paintbrushes, fill patterns, and an eraser. You might think of it as an ancestor to Photoshop.

Although it was a lot of fun to use, MacPaint was very limited. It could only create:

- Black and white pictures (no grays, no colors)
- Pixels were one size only—$1/72$ of an inch (72 ppi, pixels per inch, dots on the screen)

This wasn't all MacPaint's fault: The only Macintoshes at the time were black-and-white, and they all had screens that were 72 pixels per inch. There were no color printers, anyway, to print color images on.

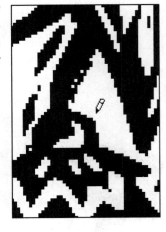

This is royalty-free clip art from Dynamic Graphics.

Notice how a picture made with MacPaint is really a collection of little black and white tiles (shown in enlargement).

Then the Mac got bigger and colorful. Photoshop came along. It could work with pixel tiles that were much "smarter" and could be shaded gray or color. Many graphics created on the Mac are of this type. Pixel-based graphics are commonly referred to as:

- Paint images
- Bitmapped images
- Raster images

All those terms mean the same thing. It means the graphic has pixels. **It is like a tiled wall.**

Now, to make it more confusing, people often use very technical terms to describe the colors of the tiles available in an image. Here's a table of terms to remember. Read the explanation of bit depth on page 30.

Colors in the Image	Terms	Bit Depth
2 (Black and White)	Line Art	1-bit
256 (usually Grays)	Grayscale or Indexed Color	8-bit
16.7 Million Colors	RGB Color or Full Color	24-bit

Most of the hotshots use **bit depth** to describe the number of colors available. To those people, a graphic is **1-**, **8-**, or **24-bit**.

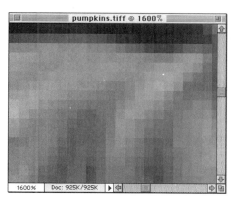

Adobe Photoshop, Adobe PhotoDeluxe, and anything called "Paint" (such as ClarisPaint, Super-Paint) create pixel-based, bitmapped images.

These days, paint style graphics can have much smarter pixel tiles. Instead of being able to understand only one bit of information, which tells the pixel to be black or white (on or off), each pixel now can understand up to 24 bits of information. Those 24 bits of information can be arranged in 16.7 million different ways, providing an image with 16.7 million colors.

An Image as a Description of Shapes

Images as shapes

Adobe Illustrator, Macromedia FreeHand, CorelDraw, and any other program with the word "Draw" in it are applications that create object-oriented (vector) images.

The other type of graphics you can create, instead of bitmapped images, have no tiles in them at all. Instead, the pictures are made of **descriptions.**

If you and I were talking on the phone and I wanted you to draw a picture of a house, I might say something like:

First, get a piece of notebook paper and turn it sideways.

Then, in the middle of the page draw a box four inches on each side.

Next, make a small dot, centered, one inch above the top of the box.

Now, make a triangle that includes the dot and the top line of the box.

You get the idea. This is very similar to what happens when your computer talks to your printer when printing these types of graphics.

This can be much more efficient than trying to say something like:

Divide up the paper into ten thousand little squares.
Make the first square white, the second square white, the third square black . . . and so on.

Pictures that use described shapes are commonly called:

- Draw-type graphics
- Object-oriented graphics
- Vector graphics

PostScript: the language of choice

When your computer talks to your printer, it doesn't use English to describe objects and text sitting on the page. Instead, it uses a special language called PostScript. PostScript is a language designed exclusively for the purpose of describing pictures on paper.

Here's a circle created in Adobe Illustrator, along with part of its PostScript description.

```
        /gt38? mark {version cvr
cvx exec} stopped {cleartomark
true} {38 gt exch pop} ifelse def

        userdict /deviceDPI 72 0
matrix defaultmatrix dtransform
dup mul exch dup mul add sqrt put

        userdict /level2?

        systemdict /languagelevel
known  dup
```

Why Shapes are Better than Dots

Small files, big resolution

Let's say you have a laser printer that is capable of 600 dpi output. When the computer sends a description of a circle to the printer, the printer receives the instructions and interprets them. Soon it starts melting little black plastic dots onto the paper and we end up with a nice 600 dpi circle.

Now, one of the cool things about PostScript is that if you print a graphic on a 300 dpi printer it comes out 300 dpi. Send the same image to a 2400 dpi imagesetter, it comes out at 2400 dpi.

So the PostScript text file that describes the circle takes up 6K on disk, yet can print at 2400 dpi. If you were to try and make the same image in the computer using pixels, a 2400 dpi circle like this would take more than *six megabytes* of disk space!

Shapes are often easier to manipulate

With vector images (shapes), if someone says, "Let's make that circle a little bigger," all you have to do is select the shape with one click, then drag on a corner to make it larger. With raster images (dots), you have to select all the individual pixels that make up the circle, and then use a scaling command. Even after that, the circle may get distorted, or it may even be impossible to separate the circle from its background in the first place.

©1994 THOMAS • BRADLEY Illustration & Design

Here's an unusual example of vector-based art that looks like a photograph. It took the artist dozens of hours to make it, and it consists of thousands of little shapes all piled on top of each other to create the illusion of something real.

Why Dots are Better than Shapes

Photorealism

While programs like Illustrator and FreeHand are great at logos, maps, and other things that are obviously graphics, creating something that looks like it's real is very difficult in an object-oriented (vector) application. It can be done much more easily with pixels.

Special effects

Certain effects can only be achieved by moving pixels around. For example, to create a sense of action, you can apply a motion blur filter in Photoshop (shown below). This type of effect is practically impossible to do in an object-oriented program.

It's very hard to create effects like this motion blur in a drawing program.

File Formats Made Easy

Go Native if You Can

Every program has what's called a **native format.** Photoshop usually saves to its very own (native) Photoshop format. Generally, other programs can't open or use files saved this way; only the application that created the native file can open or use the native file. This holds true for Illustrator, FreeHand, PageMaker, and almost every other application.

As a general rule, when you create something and **Save As...,** the format defaults to the native format.

You want to use this type of format as much as possible because native formats tend to hold the most information, and they also typically open and save the fastest.

Okay, so why are there all those other choices? The easiest answer is that native formats are often *too exclusive.* If I have a picture saved in the native Photoshop format, and I give it to someone who wants to open it in FreeHand or Illustrator, they can't. The person on the receiving end can only open it up again if they have Photoshop!

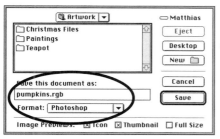

Here's Photoshop saving an image to its ***native*** *format.*

Interchange Formats

What we need are formats that lots of programs can use. That makes it easy to use a graphic in many different applications.

The file formats that allow us to open the same picture in more than one program are called **interchange** formats, and there are dozens of these formats in wide use today.

The Biggies: TIFF and EPS

TIFF (Tagged Image File Format) is the most widely used and recognized file format for bitmapped graphics, images made of *pixels* or *dots.*

EPS (Encapsulated PostScript) is the most widely used and recognized file format for vector graphics, images made of *objects* or *shapes.* Internally, an EPS file consists of a PostScript text file that describes all the objects in the illustration for printing, and a small, bitmapped rendering of the graphic so the picture can be seen on the monitor.

*This rule of thumb applies to graphics that are going to be **printed.** Color images to be printed should be saved in CMYK mode.*

*Graphics that are meant to be viewed on the **screen,** as on a web page or presentation, are a different story. Graphics on the screen should always be RGB color; GIF graphics use Indexed Color mode.*

Here's a good rule of thumb:

> If you are working with **pixels (raster images)** and want to save the image in a format that others can use it, save it as a **TIFF** file.

> If you are working with **objects (vector images)** and want to save the image in a format that others can use it, save it as an **EPS** file.

> [If you want to use the graphic on the **World Wide Web,** save it as a **GIF** or **JPEG.** Most illustrated images with areas of flat color are best saved as GIFs, and most photographs with subtle color changes are best saved as JPEGs. For a GIF, change the mode to Indexed Color and save it at the lowest bit depth (lowest number of colors) that will maintain the image. Both GIF and JPEG are raster formats.]

Bitmapped EPS files?

Pixel-based images, such as scanned graphics, can also be saved in the EPS format. These are sometimes called **bitmapped EPS** files. Many people think saving a graphic this way turns the dots into objects. It does not! The EPS file simply acts as a "shell" for a TIFF.

As a general rule, saving a scan as an EPS does not give you any advantage over saving it as a TIFF. In fact, it usually just complicates things. A scan is still a "tiled wall," even if you save it as an EPS.

Save scanned images as TIFF files. Read more about scanning your images on the following pages.

Get Great Scans

Get the Right Resolution

There is probably no greater waste of disk space and processing time in the country today than that caused by people over-scanning their photographs.

It seems logical that if you have a laser printer that prints 600 dpi, then you should scan your photos at 600 dpi. You want to take full advantage of your printer's resolution right? Well . . . this is true, but *for one-bit line art only!* Line art is made of black and white pixels. Your laser printer prints black dots on white paper, so when printing line art this one-to-one relationship works great.

With photos, it's way different. A black-and-white photo has gray areas. Your laser printer or inkjet printer (even high-end imagesetters) *cannot print gray.* All they can print are block dots on white paper. Printers **halftone** photographs to *simulate* grays, tricking your eyes into *thinking* they are seeing gray.

Here's a photo with real* grays.

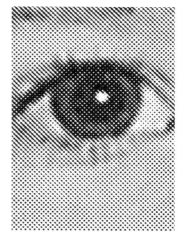

Here's the same photo, up close, after a 600 dpi laser printer halftoned it. Noticed how you can see the dots up close. Farther away, your eye cannot distinguish the individual dots and you think you see gray areas, as in the photo to the left. With a magnifying glass, look at any photo on any printed page, and you will see the dots.

*Okay, I'm lying. The printing press that printed this book can't really do gray either—it simply halftoned this photo much better than a laser printer can. It fools your eye better. But take a look at a real photograph from a camera, and notice there are no dots, just smooth blends of colors and grays.

Scanning resolution tips

Ever notice how laser-printed photos don't look so good? They look as if they are printed at a lower resolution. Well, in a sense they are. In fact, any black-and-white printer that halftones does such a bad job of reproducing grays in photos that *you can scan your photos at a much lower resolution without sacrificing any print quality at all*.

Here's a (very) rough guide to the optimal dots per inch at which to scan photos, depending on what printer you'll be using. If you are planning to scan at 100 percent size and print your scans at the same size as the original photos, this should do the trick.

Black-and-White Printer Resolution	Optimal Photo Scanning Resolution
300 dpi	100 dpi
600 dpi	150 dpi
1200 dpi	170 dpi

If you really want to know about all this resolution, frequency, and halftoning stuff, read Real World Scanning and Halftones, *by David Blatner and Steve Roth. It covers everything you could ever want to know about getting scanned images to look and print right.*

These figures are based on the default "line screen value," or lines per inch (lpi), that a laser printer uses to halftone photographs. For instance, a 300 dpi laser printer uses a 53 line per inch frequency. The scanning resolutions in the table above assume you are going to reproduce the job from the copy you output from your laser printer. *If that's what you're doing, skip the rest of this page!*

If you plan to print your job on a high-quality printing press, you have to know more about how to prepare your scan. The pros base scanning resolution on the *halftone screen frequency,* plus the *final size* of the photo in the layout.

The basic rule of thumb is: **double the screen frequency (lpi) to find the scanning resolution (dpi).** To find out what the screen frequency, or lines per inch, should be, you must ask the pressperson who will be printing the final job (the pressperson at the *print shop,* not the *service bureau* that will output the pages). Let's say they tell you the line screen will be 133 lpi. Following the rule of thumb, images printed at 133 lpi should be scanned at 266 dpi. When you output the pages at the imagesetter, be sure to tell them the required lpi. Most layout programs let you set the lpi in the Print or Page Setup dialog boxes.

If all this lpi and dpi and screen frequency talk has your head spinning, don't worry about it. It's mostly for people who are preparing documents to be output on high-end imagesetters and reproduced on printing presses.

Why Brightness and Contrast are Evil

Lots of people scan photos. The problem is, hardly anyone prepares them correctly for printing. Even professional graphics types with years of experience often don't know the two most important things that can be done to make a scan better.

The biggest problem with desktop scanners is that they are notoriously bad at capturing the darker areas of a photo—the scanner sees the darker pixels as all being pretty much the same. The result is that overall, almost all scanned photos look too dark. Almost all scans need some type of tonal adjustment to correct this darkness problem.

To correct this, most people immediately run for the Contrast and Brightness controls in their scanning software or in Photoshop.

This is a big mistake! Here's the reason why: When you use the Brightness control to make the photo lighter, you are telling every pixel in the photo to get brighter by the same amount. This is bad because pixels that were already pretty light can get "clipped"—they get turned white! The other problem is that the dark pixels don't just need lightening, they need more contrast. Since all the dark pixels are lightened by the same amount, there is no real enhancement.

The Contrast control makes the pixels different, but it's dumb about how it does it: adding contrast inadvertently clips both dark and light areas, sending pixels unnecessarily to black and white. In addition, while it enhances the dark areas, it adversely affects the light areas.

Why Levels are Good

Here's what the gurus do instead. They use Photoshop's **Levels** command instead of the Brightness and Contrast command.

Whoa! Does this mean you have to buy Photoshop? Probably not. Most scanners sold over the past few years come with Photoshop LE, which is a limited version of Photoshop that includes the Levels feature. If you're a PageMaker 6.0 or 6.5 user, check your install CD for this version of Photoshop—it's included there as well.

Let's discuss what you can do to get professional results quickly, using Levels. Let's take a look at a scanned photo, and see how we can enhance it with this command.

This scanned photo is too dark.

To the left is a photograph just after scanning. No enhancement has been done yet.

Let's pretend this scan is a bathroom tiled wall, and for some reason all the tiles have fallen on the floor. If we pick them up and sort them into stacks based on their shade, here's what we'd end up with:

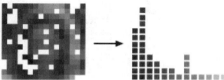

This wall had lots of dark tiles, hardly any light tiles, and some tiles in the middle (midtones).

Okay, what if we open this photo in Photoshop and use the Levels command? We get a dialog box that depicts almost identically the same thing:

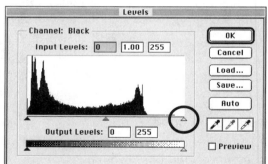

The white triangle tells which pixels in the image should turn white.

Now comes the fun part. We are going to use the Levels command to modify the brightness values of each pixel so that the photo looks great. First, we're going to readjust the white point (the lightest pixel in the image). All we have to do is drag the triangle on the right (shown above) over to the left until it starts to touch the edge of the "mountain" of pixels. This tells the scan to make just the very lightest pixels in the image white. *The entire image will now get lighter* without any significant clipping.

In some cases, you may have a photo that's too light or that lacks contrast. In that case, you'd apply the same maneuver to the black triangle way over on the left: drag it to the right until it touches the edge of the "mountain."

Another adjustment the pros do is move the middle triangle. This triangle marks where the neutral, in-the-middle, gray pixels are. The effect is to increase contrast in the light or dark areas, depending on which way you drag it. You should almost always drag this over to the left; this enhances the contrast in the dark areas only. It also brightens the entire image a bit more. How far do you drag it? It depends on the scan. Trial and error will answer the question. A good guesstimate is about halfway to the left.

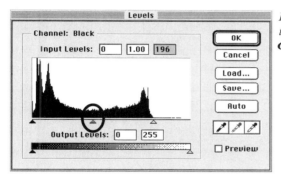

*Dragging the middle triangle is called a **Gamma** adjustment.*

Important:
*When you're talking to your techie friends, refer to the middle triangle as **Gamma**. I just showed you how to make a **Gamma Adjustment**. Throw that phrase around at a party and you'll be an instant hit.*

Here's the photo after adjustment:

Why the Pros Use Photoshop

Here's a weird problem. Let's say you have the best scanner and the best printer in the world. You also have a beautiful original photo. After you scan, adjust the Levels, and print, the printed photo always looks a little blurry compared to the original.

The process of scanning and halftone printing introduces this blurriness automatically, and there's no way to prevent it from happening! Experts love to debate why this happens, but they've come to no conclusions yet. I don't really care why it happens. What I care about is how to fix it.

Most people try to get around the blurriness by scanning their photos at a higher resolution. This usually has no effect at all because, as I discussed previously, most people are already over-scanning their photos.

So what the heck do we do about this problem? Here's what the experts do: they run a special filter called **Sharpening** on their scanned photos, and it tricks the human eye into believing the printed photo is less blurred.

A scan before and after sharpening.

Unsharp Mask

Sharpening simply accentuates edges; it makes edges more obvious by fiddling with the pixels sitting on the edge. It makes the light pixels on an edge even lighter, and the dark pixels darker. Sharpening makes the scan crisper and can compensate for the blurriness problem.

This is another place where Photoshop and Photoshop LE are way superior to every other pixel-pushing software package. While most scanning applications have a Sharpen command which works, well . . . okay, Photoshop has the **Unsharp Mask** command that is much better.

Other Sharpening commands have no setting controls, which means you can't affect how much sharpening is done. Unsharp Mask has three control areas and is much smarter than the other programs at finding edges. This is one of the main reasons the pros use Photoshop. The only reason some people avoid the Unsharp Mask command is that it's kind of intimidating. So let's take a look at it.

The Unsharp Mask command accentuates edges in a photo.

Normal edge up-close.   *Sharpened edge.*

Unsharp means Sharpen? *Okay, it's a confusing command. Just remember that Unsharp Mask **doesn't unsharpen anything, and it doesn't mask anything** either. The name Unsharp Mask comes from an old, non-digital photo-graphic process that accentuated edges in photos.*

Let's take a look at the Unsharp Mask dialog box and see how we can make it easier to understand.

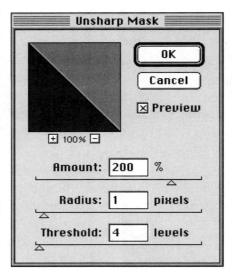

The Unsharp Mask dialog box looks scary—lots of numbers to enter. Fortunately, you only have to think hard about one of them.

Amount simply controls *how much* sharpening will be done; in other words, how much lighter will the light pixels on the edge become, and how much darker will the dark pixels be pushed. The highest number you can enter is 500, the lowest is 1. The numbers don't really mean anything special; they're just an arbitrary measure of intensity. Most experts use a number hovering around 200.

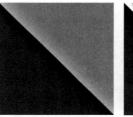

Notice how the Amount setting controls how much darker and lighter an edge is moved.

Amount 100   *Amount 200*

Let's move down to the **Threshold** area. Threshold is where you tell Photoshop *how sensitive* it should be about what it sees as an edge. If you set the number to zero, it's as sensitive as it can possibly be. At zero, Photoshop thinks almost everything is an edge! If you set it to ten, pixels side by side have to be different by ten shades of gray for it to be considered an edge. At ten, there will be very, very few edges detected in an image. Most experts use a threshold setting of three or four.

Radius is the only number that's a little tough to figure out—this is when you have to do some math. The radius setting determines how many pixels out from the edge should be darkened or lightened. As a general rule, an image that was scanned at a higher resolution needs a higher radius than an image scanned at a lower resolution.

To figure out what number to use, take the resolution of the scan and divide by 200. So if you have a photo scanned at 150 dpi, the Radius value should be .75 (150 divided by 200). Hmmm . . . what's so tough about that?

Here's what complicates things. *The resolution you scan at is often not the final resolution.* Let's say you scan a small photo at 300 dpi, and bring it into PageMaker or XPress. If you resize the photo on the page, you *change the resolution.* If you stretch a 300 dpi scan so it's twice as big, it sits on the page at 150 dpi. Shrink it to half the size? It's now 600 dpi. This final on-the-page dpi is the value to use to determine the Radius amount for Unsharp Mask.

The bigger the Radius number, the larger the edge area is.

Low Radius *High Radius*

Important note: *You really should not resize the image once it gets to your layout page—make like a pro and figure out as closely as possible what the final size of the image will be, and resize it in your image-editing software.*

So, even if you have a great scanner and a great original, you need to run Unsharp Mask on all your photo scans. This is one of the tools the pros use all the time.

Important Things to Remember

- All graphics are either made of pixels or objects (dots or shapes).

- Pixel-based graphics are made of dots and can be thought of as tiled walls. They are called paint, bitmapped, or raster graphics.

- Object-oriented graphics are shapes made of mathematical descriptions, and are called draw or vector graphics.

- PostScript is the language most often used by Macs to describe objects to laser printers and imagesetters.

- Native file formats are typically the best formats to use when saving graphics.

- If you can't use the native format and you have a bitmapped image, use the TIFF format.

- If you can't use the native format and you have an object-oriented image, use the EPS format.

- Scan black-and-white line art at a resolution that matches your black-and-white printer.

- Scan photos at a much lower resolution than line art.

- All scanned photos need correction in the tonal values and they need sharpening.

- If you have Photoshop, use the Levels command instead of the Contrast and Brightness command for correcting the tonal values.

- If you have Photoshop, use the Unsharp Mask command to sharpen scanned photos.

Managing Your Fonts 10

Manage Your Fonts the Way the Gurus Do

Okay, you may be asking yourself "What's the big deal about fonts anyway? You type something, go to the Font menu, choose one, and print it, right? I mean why are there so many books, articles, and software utilities dedicated to this stuff?"

If that's what you're thinking, you are a very lucky person and **you don't need to read this chapter!** You are probably one of those many computer users who never has to install or manage multiple fonts, or take a document created in one office across town to another office to be printed. You probably get to print your stuff on the same printer every day and use the same fonts regularly. Luckily, Apple has made life pretty easy for those of us in this position.

It tends to get a lot more complex for those folks who are design, typographic, or marketing professionals. They often have to install and manage various font libraries. They also have to create documents on one computer, send them to another computer for editing and adjustment, and finally transfer them to a totally different computer (often miles away) for printing.

These people often use **service bureaus.** Service bureaus are companies that buy expensive imagesetters (high-resolution printers) and color printers and charge you to print your stuff out on them. While this is much cheaper than buying an $80,000 printer yourself, it can be a real hassle if you don't manage your fonts in just the right way.

This chapter goes beyond the basics of handling fonts. If you're still reading, I'm going to assume you are one of those people who has to work in a complex environment where you're transferring documents between computers, using a lot of different typefaces, and maybe dealing with an outside organization like a service bureau for printing.

This is the type of environment where you need to choose the right type of fonts, organize them the right way, and use the right utility programs. You also need to recognize that things will still go wrong, and you should know how to fix them.

Do What the Experts Do

The Little Mac Book describes how fonts work. This chapter describes how experts work with fonts. I'm going to assume you are using System 7.1 or later, as some of these techniques are different with System 7.0 and earlier.

There is an amazing amount of consensus among the Mac gurus about how to handle fonts, especially among those who do a lot of publishing and graphics work. Many of these approaches fly in the face of how Apple originally designed things. Here's what I mean:

- The experts use PostScript fonts, not Apple's TrueType fonts.
- The experts all use Adobe Type Manager.
- The experts avoid using the Fonts folder.

Why is this so? Read on, and all will be revealed.

Commercial Message: You can learn much more about fonts in *How to Boss Your Fonts Around,* by Robin Williams, from Peachpit Press.

Why Experts Prefer PostScript Fonts

Printing devices fall into one of two categories: printers with a brain of their own and printers who rely on your Mac's brain.

Smart printers: Printers with a brain are usually called **PostScript printers.** These printers have a powerful processor chip inside them, and they understand **PostScript** —a special language created by Adobe Systems that is very good at describing how type and graphics should look on paper.

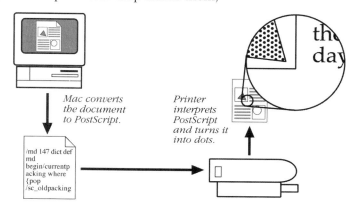

Mac converts the document to PostScript.

Printer interprets PostScript and turns it into dots.

When you print to a PostScript printer, the Mac sends a description of what it wants to have printed, and the printer understands the description and turns it into dots on the page.

Not-so-smart printers: Often called **QuickDraw printers,** these are usually inkjet devices like the StyleWriter and some inexpensive laser printers. They make your Mac do the conversion of shapes into dots and your Mac tells the printer where on the page to put the dots.

Non-PostScript printers are generally pretty slow, tie up your Mac with a lot of extra processing, and are incapable of printing the complex graphics that programs like FreeHand and Illustrator create. Many non-PostScript printers can't even print gray items, such as screened-back text or graphics.

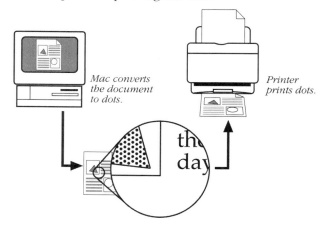

Mac converts the document to dots.

Printer prints dots.

Because of the vastly superior output quality, design professionals prefer PostScript printers. For these reasons, service bureaus have chosen PostScript printers as their standard.

PostScript Fonts vs. TrueType Fonts

What makes life confusing is that there are two major types of fonts you can install, and the different types of printers prefer one type of font over the other.

While PostScript printers can theoretically work with both types of fonts, the reality is that using anything but PostScript fonts with Post-Script printers is asking for trouble. The printer may take forever to output the document, or in some cases may fail completely. Even if your lowly laser printer can handle these other fonts, imagesetters and other complex service bureau devices typically "choke" when trying to print them. In any case, using a TrueType font on a Post-Script printer will at the very least slow down the printing process.

Another compelling reason to use PostScript fonts is that non-PostScript printers (inkjets, etc.) have no problem printing PostScript fonts. All you have to do is install the Adobe Type Manager utility (called ATM, which I describe later in this chapter).

So if you plan on printing to a PostScript printer, use only PostScript fonts. If you are using a StyleWriter or other non-PostScript printer, TrueType fonts are great (and cheaper to buy), but the combination of PostScript fonts and Adobe Type Manager can also work fine.

PostScript Fonts

Futura Condensed

This is a suitcase file. The only thing the Mac allows you to put in a suitcase are bitmapped fonts or TrueType fonts.

PostScript fonts (also called Type 1 fonts) **have two parts.** One is the **bitmapped screen font,** which is often contained in a suitcase file (called a "suitcase" file because the icon looks like a little suitcase). Screen fonts are made of little pixel paintings, designed to be easily read on a computer screen. The little pixels are configured to line up with the pixels on your monitor, which makes them look nice on the screen. The biggest reason you need the bitmapped **screen font** is so the font will appear in your menu and display on the **screen.**

The second part of a PostScript font is the outline **printer font,** which consists of PostScript outlines that describe the letter shapes. This is the part the **printer** needs so it can print the font.

You have to have both parts to be able to see a font on screen and to print it! And both of those parts must be stored in the correct place.

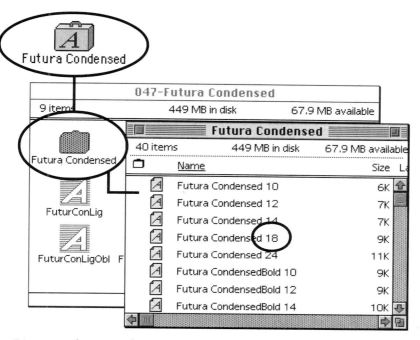

Bitmapped screen fonts are created in specific sizes, which is why they are also called *fixed-size fonts*. You can tell which files are screen fonts because their name displays their size (as shown above). Bitmaps generally live in suitcase files (although they can exist outside of suitcase files as well). If you are using ATM, you only need *one* of these fixed sizes per font. For instance, if you have the Times family with Times Regular, Times Italic, Times Bold, and Times Bold Italic, you only need four files in your suitcase. I tend to keep an 18- or 24-point size in my suitcases, if they are available; otherwise I keep the 12-point size.

RubinSanICGFil

UtopiReg

Printer fonts have a wide range of icons. Often there is a number 1 in the icon, to indicate a PostScript Type 1 font.

This is an example of an outline contained in a printer font.

Printer fonts have a variety of icons. The printer font, also known as an outline font, contains the PostScript mathematical formula that outlines the shapes of the letters.

TrueType fonts have 3 letters A's on their icons. You only need this one icon for TrueType to appear on your screen and to print.

You will also probably find bitmap versions of your TrueType faces. These are unnecessary; they're meant for speed, but the speed increase is negligible. You can toss them if you are sure they are the bitmaps that belong to TrueType fonts.

TrueType Fonts

TrueType fonts can also be stored in suitcases. **TrueType fonts have only one part—the outline printer part.** The Mac knows how to convert (called "rasterize") these outlines into on-screen renditions when needed. This is kind of neat. It means TrueType fonts don't ever look "jaggy" on your monitor. Your Mac can rasterize the outline for your screen at any size, using the outlines to create the bitmapped screen fonts on the fly.

As it turns out, **it is possible to do the same thing with PostScript fonts.** You just have to install Adobe Type Manager, and it will turn the outline-based printer fonts into screen fonts when you don't have the right screen font size installed. This action of turning shapes into dots is usually called **rasterizing.** You'll hear this term used a lot by people who are really into graphics and publishing. When your PostScript laser printer converts outline letter shapes into dots on paper, that's also called rasterizing.

What About QuickDraw GX Fonts?

You may have something called QuickDraw GX installed on your Mac. This is an advanced printing system created by Apple that has (so far) received little to no support from developers and thus clouds the whole font management issue. Sometimes this obscure printing software has been turned on by accident. Odds are that you can disengage it without losing any important features. Unless you consciously choose to use the GX system and the GX fonts and you understand all about them, you should probably open your Extensions Manager and make the GX Extension inactive. We won't be covering QuickDraw GX here as it only muddies the font waters and very, very few people use it.

Why Experts Use Adobe Type Manager

Adobe Type Manager (or ATM for short) was introduced in 1988. It quickly became a standard item in every Mac professionals' System Folder. Here's why:

ATM Makes PostScript Type Look Great on the Screen

Bitmapped fonts, also called fixed-size fonts, are created to display certain point sizes of type on the screen as clearly as possible. Without ATM installed, when you choose a PostScript font size for which a specific bitmap size has not been created, the Mac takes an existing bitmap size and "tweaks" it to make it work. The results are ugly.

(Of course, the *printer* always prints the *printer outline* font, not the bitmap *screen* font, so on paper it prints just fine. It just looks horrible on the screen.)

 *Without ATM, you'll get ugly jaggies on screen if you don't have the right screen font size loaded. In fact, even if you have the screen font size installed, it doesn't look as good as when ATM rasterizes the outline.*

When you choose an odd font size with ATM installed, ATM finds the printer outline and uses that outline to create a clean image of the letters for your screen.

 *ATM rasterizes printer font outlines for much smoother type on the screen and on non-PostScript printers.*

ATM Makes Type Print Great on Non-PostScript Printers

Let's say you're using a PostScript font like Futura, and you try printing it to your StyleWriter or DeskJet printer. Without ATM, the printer freaks out and tells your Mac, "Forget it—I don't DO PostScript!" and you get a really jagged printout.

ATM will convert (rasterize) the PostScript outlines for the printer, at whatever resolution the printer happens to be, and the type will then look great!

SuperATM Can Create "Synthetic" Fonts When Needed

A few years ago Adobe introduced SuperATM, which has a very cool feature. Imagine someone gave you an electronic document that used a font (let's say Garamond) you didn't have installed on your computer. Normally, the file would open and your Mac would substitute Courier for the missing font.

jitters?

This is true Garamond.

jitters?

This is a synthetic font generated by ATM to match the metrics of Garamond. Notice the difference in the letters and especially the question mark. Also notice how well ATM emulated Garamond.

Not only is Courier an ugly typeface, but all your page and line breaks change because Courier letters have different metrics (that is, different widths and spacing adjustments) than Garamond.

With SuperATM installed, instead of substituting Courier the program creates a "temporary version" of Garamond (or any other Adobe font) with the same metrics as the original font! Although the type doesn't look exactly like *true* Garamond, the document maintains the same line and page breaks, the same weight and style specifications, and the same proportions as the original font. When the document goes back to the computer it was created on, or any computer with the original font, it transforms back into that original font.

The one drawback is that this substitution only works with Adobe-brand fonts. The good news is that ATM version 4.0 has this capability built-in, so you don't have to pay extra for SuperATM anymore.

ATM Can Manage Font Libraries

Adobe Type Manager Deluxe is enhanced so that it can manage font libraries. This is a fancy way of saying that you don't have to put fonts into the Font folder to make them work, and you don't have to have all of your fonts loaded all the time (which can make your font menu unwieldy and drag down the System performance). Managing your font library is described in much more detail in the next section of this chapter.

Why the Experts Use a Font Management Program Instead of the Fonts Folder

The Problem

The standard method of installing a font, according to Apple, is to drag the screen and printer fonts into your Fonts folder, which lives in your System Folder. It's easy, it works, and it's free. So why do the experts avoid doing it this way?

There are several major limitations to using the Fonts folder.

The Fonts Folder has a capacity limit. You can only put 128 items into the folder. If you have a vast font library, you will hit this boundary fairly quickly.

The Fonts Folder cannot have subfolders within it. You cannot group your screen fonts and printer fonts together in a folder and put it into the Fonts folder. Well, you can *do* it, but your fonts won't work. This makes swapping fonts in and out of the folder very difficult. It also makes for sloppy organization.

Running applications are not updated. You must quit every open application, then install fonts into the Fonts folder, and, finally, relaunch the applications for the fonts to appear in the menus.

Startup time gets slower. The more fonts in your Fonts folder, the slower your startup time becomes.

You have to keep all your fonts on the startup disk. The Fonts folder must be on the active startup disk—you can't move the folder out of the System Folder and put it in a more convenient place.

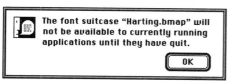

*Aack! If you add a new font to the Fonts folder, you have to quit and relaunch everything before they'll work. (What a silly message—the fonts will not be available until after the application **quits?**)*

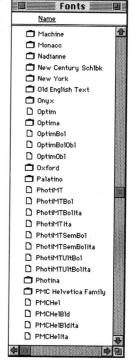

You can't put fonts into subfolders when you use the standard Mac Fonts folder— pretty messy!

The Solution: Font Management Software

Even before the Fonts folder was invented (it was implemented in System 7.1 in 1992) some clever programmers came up with software that lets you put your fonts anywhere you want, group them into folders, and overcome the 128 item limit. One useful feature of font management programs is the ability to create "font sets." Font sets let you create collections of fonts associated with particular projects. For example, with a button click you can open a set of fonts that you always use for a particular client or brochure.

There are four font management programs.

The program Suitcase (capital "S") has nothing to do with the suitcase (lowercase "s") files that you store fonts in. Just because you have suitcase icons does not mean you have the Suitcase program!

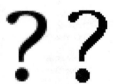

In a program like Photoshop that uses pixels, not mathematical outlines, to create type forms, the type used in images looks smoother when the edges blend into the background. This is called anti-aliasing (left). If you don't anti-alias the type, you get jagged edges (right). (On a printed page, ATM makes the type smooth without anti-aliasing.)

Suitcase from Symantec: Suitcase was the first program to let you do all these neat things. It is also (currently) the most popular font management program. In addition to all the basic goodies, it can compress fonts so they take up less disk space. It is also the only **AppleScript-able** font manager, which means a real Mac geek could write scripts to automate some procedures, like activating certain fonts with the launch of a particular document.

MasterJuggler Pro from Alsoft: MasterJuggler does almost all the things Suitcase does, except scripting, and has the added capability of identifying fonts that are corrupted. This can be a real time saver because corrupted fonts can cause major printing problems and even crashes. MasterJuggler can also detect which fonts have been used in a document and then create handy duplicates that you can put on a floppy when you have to take a document elsewhere for printing.

Some people say MasterJuggler's interface is awkward and hard to follow. Some hate the fact that there is no "Add All" button. Others argue that it's the only font manager that can also be used to launch applications. Its application launcher is so good that some people buy it just for that purpose.

ATM Deluxe from Adobe Systems: Adobe updated ATM to ATM Deluxe in early 1997 and enhanced it significantly. Everyone is already using ATM to get great-looking type on screen, but with this new version Adobe adds font management capabilities as well. ATM Deluxe also lets you anti-alias fonts on screen, like on Web pages, and can be set up to load fonts in a document automatically when you open the document. ATM can even detect font corruption.

One problem with ATM Deluxe is that you can only add entire suitcases to a set; that is, if you have individual fonts that are not in suitcase files, you will have to make suitcases for each one of them before you can add them to your font list.

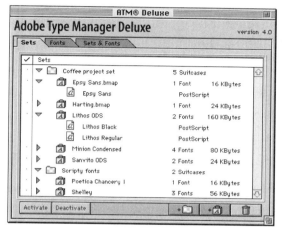

Adobe Type Manager Deluxe lets you organize your fonts by project, as well as by family, or by any other category you make up.

Font Reserve from DiamondSoft: Font Reserve is a new software program that can solve most of the font problems you ever have had or may ever have. When you initially set up the program, Font Reserve scans each font, checks for corruption, sorts them, removes duplicates, matches printer fonts with screen fonts, organizes your fonts, and gives you a report on exactly what it found and where there are problems. When you add new fonts to Font Reserve it can automatically organize them for you and put them into its Vault. Font Reserve is database-driven and keeps full information about individual fonts in its database, such as foundry, version, classification (like serif, sans serif, modern, script), plus you can sort and query the database. You don't need to deal with the physical fonts anymore—you can let Font Reserve do all the work. This is a rich and extraordinarily useful application.

Which Font Manager to Use?

Which one should you use? If you need scripting, buy Suitcase. If you have to have MasterJuggler's application launcher, buy that. If you have average font needs, use ATM Deluxe. If you own a large library of fonts and want all your problems solved, get Font Reserve.

Typical Font Problems and How to Solve Them

I have a bunch of TrueType fonts in my Mac—how do I get rid of them?

First of all, remember that using TrueType is perfectly fine for many people. If you are not taking documents to be printed elsewhere, or are only using a non-PostScript printer like the StyleWriter, you should probably just keep them.

If you fall into the PostScript camp and want to get rid of your TrueType fonts, here's how to do it:

1. Open the Fonts folder inside your System Folder.

2. Leave all suitcases with city names alone (city names such as New York, Geneva, or Monaco). Even though these suitcases probably contain TrueType fonts, your Mac really prefers that you not mess with them—the Mac uses those fonts for menus and dialog boxes. Just avoid using city-named fonts in anything you are going to print. (City-named fonts also look better on Web pages than other fonts. Try New York 12 point in your browser instead of Times 12 point.)

3. Open the other suitcases and look for font files with multiple "A"s on them—they are TrueType fonts.

4. Drag those files to the trash.

Times Courier

These are TrueType icons.

I'm using ATM, but some of my fonts look jaggy on screen.

This can happen if you are using a font for which **you don't have a matching printer outline font** or if the outline fonts are stored in the wrong place. For instance, the Fonts folder might have the screen font suitcase in it but not the matching printer font, or you may have opened a font in your font manager but ATM can't find the matching printer font because you put it in the wrong place.

The solution is to **find the printer font files** and make sure they are in the same folder as the screen font suitcase (use Find File and search for the first five characters of the font name). Every bitmap screen font *must* have a matching printer font. That is, the Garamond Regular bitmap must have the matching Garamond Regular printer font; Garamond Italic bitmap must have the matching Garamond Italic printer font. The matching screen and printer fonts must be stored together in one folder.

Another problem might be that you don't *have* the matching printer font. For instance, the outline printer fonts for the bitmaps that come with most PostScript printers (Bookman, New Century Schoolbook, Zapf Chancery, etc.) are stored in the printer's ROM. ATM can't find the outlines when they are stored in the printer's ROM, so it can't display them cleanly on the screen. They will *print* just fine because the PostScript printer *can* find the outline. The only way to make those LaserWriter ROM fonts (called "resident" fonts because they reside in the printer) rasterize on the screen is to buy the matching printer fonts. Personally, I think buying new and more interesting fonts altogether would be a better investment.

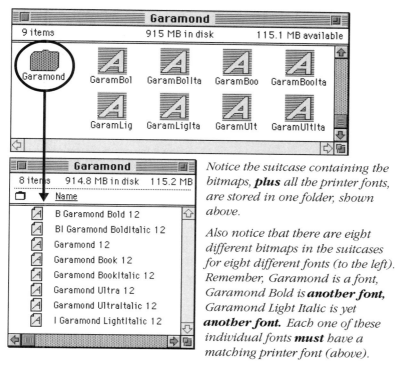

*Notice the suitcase containing the bitmaps, **plus** all the printer fonts, are stored in one folder, shown above.*

*Also notice that there are eight different bitmaps in the suitcases for eight different fonts (to the left). Remember, Garamond is a font, Garamond Bold is **another font**, Garamond Light Italic is yet **another font**. Each one of these individual fonts **must** have a matching printer font (above).*

I have a font that appears in the menu and on screen, but looks funny when it prints.

Printer fonts names almost always start with the first five characters of the screen font name. See the illustration on the previous page.

This is another situation where the screen font is loaded (activated in the System), but the printer font is missing or misplaced. Find the printer font file (search for the first five characters in the font name) and make sure the printer font and the bitmap are in the same folder.

I've got text that looks bold on screen, but doesn't print bold.

For a font to print bold, there must be a bold outline present. Zapf Chancery, for example, has no bold outline at all. Even though you can choose the "Bold" option on the menu, and it looks bold on screen, the monitor is tricking you. When you send the document to the printer, the printer tries to find a matching bold outline in its ROM chips. If the printer can't find outlines there, it asks the Mac to look on the hard disk. If the printer can't find a proper printer outline, the font just prints normal (not bold).

Find the correct outline font (if there is one) and put it in the same folder as the bitmap. If you don't have a bold outline, don't try to make the typeface bold.

I've selected the text and hit the "Italic" button, but it looks and prints awful.

zen fat
zen fat

Notice how the italic characters are not just slanted versions of the Roman face (non-italic), but have been completely redesigned. This means the italic has completely different outlines from the regular font.

Every member of a typeface family is actually a separate, individual font. The italic version of a face is not merely slanted, it has been totally redesigned by the type designer. Thus each member of a family has its own bitmap *and* its own outline printer font. Depending on how your fonts have been set up by the font vendor as well as on your machine with various font utilities, you may or may not get the true italic outline when you click the italic button in your software. If the Mac can't grab the printer outline when you click the button, it will just slant the type.

Although you can *sometimes* safely make typefaces italic or bold by hitting the keyboard shortcut or clicking a button, you will have fewer surprises and problems if you take the extra second to choose the actual bold or italic typeface from the menu. This tip is particularly important if you're going to take the publication to a service bureau.

When I'm creating a long document, I often use the keyboard short-cut to make the type italic or bold, then when I am finished I use search-and-replace to remove the italic or bold and change the type to the true italic or bold font.

Some of my letters are getting cut off.

This happens a lot in Photoshop. When you type something, ATM needs to render it on screen. It looks at what you typed and decides if it should try to render accurate line spacing or if character shapes are more important. (ATM is mostly concerned with how to adjust the screen display to show accent marks on capital letters, such as É.)

Whether it displays the line spacing or the character shapes properly is determined through ATM's preferences. The default setting is for line spacing to be preserved, which usually is best for pages of text. In the case of Photoshop type, character shapes are more important than line spacing. Open the ATM Control Panel and set it to "Preserve Character shapes" instead. You will have to restart your Mac before this preference can take effect.

golly jolly

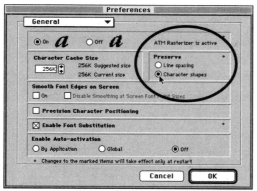

If your letters get chopped off in Photoshop, change your ATM Preferences.

When I make some of the characters in my document extra large, they turn into ugly bitmaps.

To create extra large type or if you have a large number of fonts in one publication, you may need to enlarge ATM's **cache.** Adobe recommends about 50K per font you have loaded. Make the cache change in the Control Panel. You will need to restart before the enlarged cache will take effect.

Important Things to Remember

- If you ever take files to a service bureau for printing, use only PostScript fonts.
- Always use Adobe Type Manager with PostScript fonts.
- Suitcase, MasterJuggler Pro, Adobe Type Manager Deluxe, and Font Reserve are font management programs. They let you store fonts outside the Fonts folder and load only the fonts you need when you need them.
- Make sure you keep PostScript outline fonts in the same folder as their bitmapped screen font equivalents.
- Make sure you have a printer font for every bitmap, and vice versa.
- If you're using a lot of fonts in one document, or if you're using very large sizes of fonts, increase ATM's cache.

Tips and Tricks

11

Amaze your Friends and Mystify your Enemies (and make your life easier)

This chapter is about little and not-so-little tips and tricks that long-time Mac users take advantage of all the time to make their lives easier. These are the kinds of things you can take advantage of every-day to enhance the way you use your Macintosh. Also be sure to read the plethora of tips Robin already collected in *The Little Mac Book*.

Besides all of the usual keyboard shortcuts and timesavers, I also discuss one of my favorite pieces of System software that 99 percent of Mac users (even the experts) usually ignore.

Tape Your Option Key Down

I was showing off some of the following tips at a seminar and an attendee said "Gee, those shortcuts are so handy, maybe I should just tape the Option key down!"

While that's a bit extreme, it's true that using your Option key at the right time can unlock a bunch of hidden Mac capabilities.

Close All Windows

If you hold the Option key down while you click on a close box *or* use the Command O shortcut, *all open windows in the Finder will close.* Nothing reduces desktop clutter faster than this.

Close Enclosing Windows

Another great clutter-prevention tip is to hold down the Option key when you double-click to open a folder, and *the folder window it came out of automatically closes.* Once you try this, its value becomes apparent—you'll use it all the time.

Drag-Copy

Everybody knows that when you drag something from *one disk* to *another disk,* the Mac automatically makes a copy. What if you want a copy of the *same file* on the *same disk?* You can use the Duplicate command in the File menu (Command D), of course. An easier way is to hold down the Option key and drag the file to another folder or to the Desktop—instant copy!

Switch Applications Cleanly

When you leave one program to go to another, you can use the Application menu in the far-right corner of the menu bar, or you can just click on the program window you want to activate. If you hold the Option key down while you switch applications, *the application window you're leaving will hide.*

To hide the current application while you go to the Desktop, hold down the Option key and click on the Desktop.

Trash Locked Files

How many times have you tried to empty the Trash and received the message that there's a locked item in the Trash and it can't be emptied? Hold down the Option key while you choose the Empty Trash command and *locked items will be automatically deleted*—without the annoying dialog box.

I Hate When That Happens!

There are plenty of times when your Mac tries to be *too* helpful. Often it gets in your face with unnecessary dialog boxes or bizarre requests. Here are a few of the most common irritations and how to deal with them.

When Your Mac is Acting Really Slow

Turn off "Calculate folder sizes"

The Views Control Panel includes an option called "Calculate folder sizes." When this is on, you can see how much disk space a folder takes up when you are looking at a window in list view.

Most people turn this off because the constant background recalculations really slow the computer down, even when you're not at the Desktop.

Although with every new release of Mac System software they promise they've made this feature much faster and more efficient, calculating folder sizes can still make your Mac crawl at times, particularly if you use some applications like PageMaker. If you want to know how big a folder is, just click on the folder and use the Get Info command instead.

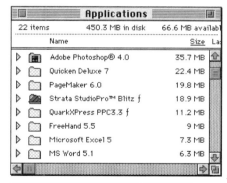

Sure, it's nice to see how much disk space folders take, but it's not worth the performance penalty.

Use the Views Control Panel to turn off "Calculate folder sizes."

Use a System font for icon views

It's really neat that you can customize your Mac so easily to look the way you want. You can change your Desktop patterns, modify icons, and color things. The bad news is that many of these changes can affect performance.

I generally tell people that it's okay to make most changes, but try to avoid changing the "Font for views" option in the Views Control Panel. The default choice, Geneva 9, is an excellent one to keep for two reasons:

- *Geneva is a "city" font, designed for easy reading on a Mac screen.* Most other fonts are designed for *printing*—not for on-screen reading. Geneva, like New York, is a font named after a city and has been optimized for easy viewing on your monitor. When you choose other fonts like Times or Palatino, slight distortions in the letter shapes make on-screen reading harder.

- *Geneva 9 is fast.* Geneva, Monaco, and Chicago fonts are built-into the Mac System software. Other choices are always going to be rendered more slowly on your monitor. In some cases, it creates a very noticeable slowdown.

Rebuild your Desktop file

When you double-click on a folder, does it take a long time for the window to open? Odds are that you need to perform the ritual of a Desktop rebuild. Hold down your **Command** and **Option** keys while **restarting** and your Mac will prompt you for a rebuild. In Chapter Five, we discuss this in more detail.

When Your Mac Tells You Stuff You Already Know

Silly Trash Messages

You've dropped something into the Trash and then you use the "Empty Trash" command under the Special Menu. Odds are a dopey dialog box will appear telling you that you're emptying the Trash!

You may have tried in the past to kill this alert by looking for a Control Panel that has a setting to turn it off. Stop hunting—you won't find one. Instead, select the Trash icon and use the "Get Info" command from the File menu, or the Command I keyboard shortcut. Uncheck the "Warn before emptying" checkbox, and it will never bother you again.

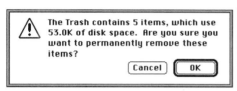

Nice of it to ask, but better to turn it off. Just click on the Trash icon, Get Info, and uncheck the warning box.

Redundant Startup Messages

Here's another silly one. When your Mac crashes and you restart it, you are faced with a dialog box informing you that you crashed!

This is easy to get rid of so you won't ever see it again. When your computer is back up and running just go to your General Controls Control Panel and uncheck the "Warn me if computer was shut down improperly" checkbox.

If you don't like being reminded of a bad crash experience, just go to your General Controls Control Panel and turn it off.

When Your Mac Asks for a Disk It Doesn't Need

What do you do when you want to eject a disk? Don't tell me you go to the Special Menu and use the Eject Disk command! It's very strange that what seems to be the best command to do something is really the worst.

The problem is that the Eject Disk command leaves a "ghost" icon that can come back to haunt you. What can happen is that the Mac thinks the ejected disk is still available. What makes things worse is that it will sometimes ask for the disk back! One quick remedy to this problem is to use the universal Macintosh "Stop That" keyboard shortcut. Of course I'm talking about **Command Period.** This will usually make your Mac stop asking for the disk.

But there's a preventative solution, and that is to eject the disk using the **Put Away** command instead of the Eject menu command! The Put Away command is in the File menu and has a simple keyboard shortcut: **Command Y.** To eject a disk, all you do is click on the disk icon, hit the Command Y shortcut, and the disk ejects leaving no ghostly residue.

Or **drag** the disk icon to the Trash (it won't Trash anything on the disk!), which accomplishes the same thing as Command Y: it ejects the disk while avoiding the "ghost."

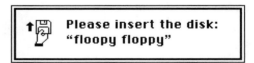

If you use the Eject Disk command, your Mac will probably ask for the disk back. Use the Put Away command or drag the disk to the Trash instead.

When Your Mac Can't See a Disk That's Really There

In this world of Zip disks and external hard drives, it's not uncommon that you will shut down your Mac, connect one of these devices, restart to mount the disk, only to find that your Mac can't see it!

The experts all use a handy little utility called **SCSIProbe** (pronounced "scuzzy probe"). Almost every time your Mac fails to see an external disk or recognize a drive, this guy will find it and make it appear.

Just open the SCSIProbe utility and it should list all the connected devices. Click the "Mount" button (or just type M), and it almost always forces hesitant disks to appear on the Desktop.

SCSIProbe is freeware; you can find it online or from your local Mac user group (see Chapter Thirteen for resources).

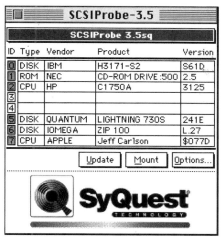

If a disk won't appear on the Desktop, SCSIProbe can often bring it out of hiding.

When Your Mac Freaks Out

It happens way too often. You'll be working along just fine, and your Mac will suddenly freeze. The cursor will just stop moving! These are commonly called crashes, lockups, or freezes. Most people just hit the power switch or pull the power plug to get going again. This, of course, causes all your applications to vanish from memory and all your unsaved work is lost forever.

Here's something to try first, before you pull the plug—it works about a third of the time. Hold down the **Command** and **Option** keys and press the **Escape** (esc) key. This is called a **Force Quit.** If you're lucky, it will bring up a dialog box that asks if you really want to force the crashed application to quit.

If you click the "Force Quit" button on that message, it sometimes makes the crashed program quit, and you can switch to other open applications and save your documents *before using the Restart command from the Special Menu.* Don't make the mistake of thinking that the Force Quit command (when it works) saves you from having to restart the computer entirely. Even though a Force Quit seems to make everything okay, you need to purge the error that caused the crash in the first place. A complete restart is the only way to do that.

*You may not have to lose everything after a crash! Sometimes a Force Quit will save the day, and you will only lose what you haven't saved in **that** program.*

Another handy keyboard shortcut to know when Force Quit fails is **Command Control PowerOn.** (The PowerOn key is the one you hit to turn on your computer; it has a little triangle on it. If you don't have a PowerOn key, you can't use this tip.) On most Macs, pressing these keys together will reboot the machine. This has the same effect of turning the computer off and then back on, but without actually cutting power to the machine.

If that keyboard shortcut doesn't work, look on your computer, perhaps around the back, for a tiny button or tab with a triangle on it. If you see one, it's the Restart button. Press it to restart.

The geeks call this a "warm boot." The interior circuitry of your Mac likes a warm boot much better than turning off the power altogether.

Smart Navigation and Launching

Where the Heck am I?

This happens all the time—you're in the Finder with a window open. The window may have a generic name like "Letters" and you wonder *which* Letters folder this is. Is this the Letters folder on my hard disk, or is this the one on my backup volume? There's no way of knowing just by looking at the title bar.

Here's what to do. Hold down your **Command key and press on the title bar** of the window. Press where the window name is and a little menu will reveal the path of folders to this window/folder location.

Another great thing about this trick is that you can *move up the hierarchy*. That is, if you Command-press to get that menu, you can select any folder in the menu and it will open the selected folder.

One trick further: if you select a folder in that menu while holding down the **Option** key, the window you were in will close before the new window opens. This is another great window-clutter-reduction technique.

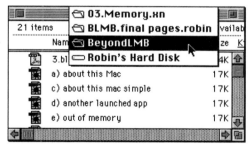

Command-press on the title bar to get this handy little menu. From the menu, select any folder to open it.

Dialog Box Shortcuts

Checkboxes and radio buttons are generally pretty small and hard to click on. You don't need to actually click on these items to make them active or inactive. *Just click on the text beside the box or button and 99 percent of the time it will work the same as if you clicked the button itself.*

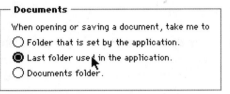

You don't have to aim for those teeny radio buttons—just click on the text next to them.

Many programs today let you use the **Escape** key (esc) on the keyboard as an equivalent for clicking on the **Cancel** button. This is sometimes a little easier than using the universal Command Period shortcut for Cancel.

When an application asks if you want to save something before closing, many times you can type the **N** key instead of clicking the "No" button. Some programs, like Photoshop, let you type a **D** for "Don't Save." Try this in your favorite applications and see if it works for you.

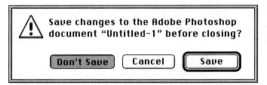

Try using your keyboard! D equals "Don't Save" in Photoshop.

Small Icons on the Desktop

By this time, you're probably already using drag-and-drop to launch documents with specific applications. For example, if someone gives you a scanned image created with Deskscan and you want to open it in Photoshop, you can just drag the document icon to the Photoshop application icon.

Drag documents onto program icons—don't just double-click and hope for the best!

Most folks take this a step further and make aliases of their favorite programs and put them on the Desktop (to make an alias, select an icon and press Command M). This not only makes launching programs easier, but also makes it easy to open documents: just drag-and-drop the document on top of the alias.

Many folks have reduced Desktop clutter by putting *small* icons on the Desktop. This is tougher than it sounds, since there is no "View by Small Icon" option for the Desktop!

There are a couple of workarounds for this. One is to get your hands on the shareware macro program **KeyQuencer.** KeyQuencer can tweak your Mac so you can view the Desktop by small icon. While this is easy, it takes practically an act of Congress to get *me* to install an Extension that isn't absolutely necessary—especially one that "tricks" my Mac into doing something it normally doesn't want to do.

Instead, I do it the old-fashioned way. I do the old paste-a-new-icon-in-the-Get-Info-window trick as Robin described in *The Little Mac Book*. I paste a **small** icon in place of the standard big icon.

The only hard part is getting your hands on the small icons. One way to do it is with Apple's **ResEdit** software, the free program that lets you extract and modify graphics and other resources from applications. If you're familiar with ResEdit, you can open the "ics8" resource for the application, then copy that into the icon editor part of the program for adjustment.

Using the old copy-and-paste icon trick, you can use a painting program to make small icons for your files on the Desktop.

But this is how I do it:

- I take a screen shot of a window while viewing the contents "By Small Icon" (press Command Shift 3 to take a screen shot).

- I open the screen shot in Photoshop, select a 32x32 pixel area (the exact size of an icon) surrounding the icon in question, and copy this small image.

- I then paste this small image into the Get Info box for the application sitting on my Desktop.

The **Command Shift 3** keyboard sequence will capture the current screen image as a snapshot and save it onto your hard disk. It saves it to a file called "Picture 1" and puts it in the root directory (the root directory is the window that opens when you double-click the hard disk icon). Subsequent snapshots are saved to the name "Picture 2," etc. If you have Photoshop, you can double-click on the marquee tool to specify a selection of 32x32 pixels. If you don't have Photoshop, you can use any simple paint program to select the small icon out of the screen shot and copy it.

My Favorite Tip: Work While You Drive

For the past year I've been telling anyone who would listen about this tip. As someone who spends a lot of time in the car, this is my favorite Macintosh timesaver.

In this age of information overload, I've discovered a way to blaze through the tons of reading material I'm faced with annually. The e-mails, faxes, Web pages, downloaded articles, and even books that used to stack up in my to-read box are now quickly dispatched. I've figured out a way to learn more while stressing a lot less.

For me, the number-one productivity application on the Macintosh is (drum roll) **SimpleText**.

SimpleText? That goofy little word processor from Apple? How can that be a major productivity enhancer? Here's the deal. Starting with System 7.0, the Macintosh came with a Text-to-Speech capability. What that means is any program (like SimpleText) that supports this System software, called PlainTalk, *can read out loud to you.*

Here's a quick way to find out if you have this Text-to-Speech software installed. Find a copy of the SimpleText application on your hard disk. Launch SimpleText and type something. Then go up to your Sound menu and look for a menu command called "Speak All."

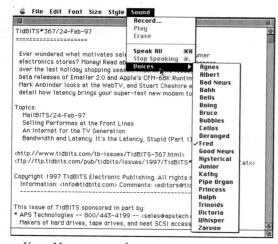

If that command is not gray, your System is configured for speech. If you choose that command and wait a few seconds, your Mac should speak what you typed.

You can even choose from different voices. I have found the default voice "Fred" to be the best combination of quality and resource efficiency (other voices can take a lot more RAM and CPU resources).

Although SimpleText works great and the price is right (free), it is limited to only working with text files that are 32K or less. If you work with larger text files than that, you may want to use ClarisWorks instead.

Your Mac can read to you with many different voices— most people prefer Fred for easy listening.

Teaching ClarisWorks to Speak

Here's how to set up ClarisWorks so it can speak text:

- Open a word processing document in ClarisWorks.

- From the File menu, choose "Shortcuts," and slide over to the "Edit Shortcuts" submenu. This will bring up a dialog box that shows all the shortcuts available.

- Scroll down the Shortcuts list until you see an icon that looks like a pair of lips; this represents the "Speak Text" feature (see below).

- Double-click on that lips icon and it will be added to your standard Shortcuts palette. Click OK to close the dialog box.

- Now, go back to the File menu and choose "Shortcuts" again, and slide over to the "Show Shortcuts" submenu. This will bring up a floating Shortcuts palette.

- Highlight some text in your document, then click on the lips in the palette. It should now speak the selection.

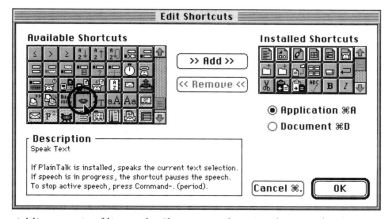

Adding a pair of lips to the Shortcuts palette in ClarisWorks will enable that program to talk as well as SimpleText.

If Speech Doesn't Work

If the speech commands don't work, here's what you must do to add this capability to your Macintosh. There are four main components that need to be installed in your System Folder:

- The **Speech Control Panel** in the Control Panels folder
- The **Speech Manager Extension** in the Extensions Folder
- The **MacinTalk Extension** in the Extensions Folder
- The **Voices folder** in the Extensions Folder

Most of the Macs I've encountered have these items readily available on the hard disk. Often, the Extensions Manager has been used to disengage these components. Check there first to see if you can reactivate them. If not, you'll need to install from scratch.

The System disks that came with your Mac may have these speech programs available for installation. Most System CDs have them listed as "PlainTalk" components or "Text-to-Speech" components. Try launching the System Installer program and see if they're available.

Many Macs that came with the System software on floppies will not have these components available. Luckily, the Apple Web site allows you to download the software for free. Look for it at *http://speech. apple.com/ptk/ptk.html*.

SimpleText, WordPerfect, and ClarisWorks are examples of programs that can take advantage of this System software. Word cannot.

How to Use the Talking Feature

Some PowerBook users I know just open up the machine, plop it in the passenger seat, crank up the volume on the internal speakers, and let it read while they drive (you need a pretty quiet car for this). Others plug a pair of Walkman-type headphones into the Power-Book sound-out port and listen that way.

Since in many states listening to headphones while driving is illegal (not to mention potentially dangerous), I prefer to transcribe the sound files onto cassette. For desktop-Mac users, this is your only option. At stores like Radio Shack you should be able to find a cable that will interface from your stereo sound-out port on your Mac into a tape recorder. This makes it easy to create cassettes that you can listen to while driving, mowing the lawn, or doing the dishes.

It's great! I just "read" the most recent issue of *Macworld* (down-loaded from their Web site) while I drove to work this morning!

Some people find these voices too mechanical and don't like listen-ing to them. Others have quickly gotten used to it and don't mind at all. Try it out!

One Last Point

While it's theoretically possible for a Windows machine to read to you, it's so hard to set up that no one actually does it. I use this as ammunition all the time when I'm involved in the age-old Windows/Mac debate. I just say something like "I'd consider switching, but I need a computer that will read my e-mail messages to me while I'm driving."

Important Things to Remember

- Hold your Option key down when closing and opening windows to reduce window clutter.

- For maximum computing speed, use the View Control Panel to turn off the "Calculate folder sizes" option, and use Geneva 9 for your standard views font.

- Get Info on the Trash and turn off the "Warn before emptying" checkbox.

- Use the General Controls Control Panel to turn off the "improper shut down" warning.

- Always use the Put Away command instead of the Eject Disk command.

- SCSIProbe can make hesitant disks appear on the Desktop.

- Command Option Escape can sometimes force a crashed application to quit.

- Clicking on the text adjacent to checkboxes is a lot easier than clicking on the checkboxes themselves.

- Put commonly used application aliases on the Desktop for drag-and-drop launching.

- Try out the Text-to-Speech option in SimpleText and ClarisWorks.

Get on the Web

12

There is a Lot to Do There!

What does getting "on the Web" mean? A simple answer would be that it means looking at Web pages. It means using special software called a Web browser in conjunction with (usually) a modem to view special pages that are "served" up by computers all over the world. Some people call this "surfing" the Web.

An expert would say that surfing Web pages is just a small part of the entire Internet experience. They'd say that understanding e-mail, getting on mailing lists, joining discussion groups, and "chatting" are significant too. All those things are neat, but I'd like you to just **focus on the surfing** part at first. If you are new to all this Internet stuff, and you want to get involved, this is the place to start.

The Internet is a big, complex subject, and it can be very confusing. I've found that beginners who establish a strong foothold in just the surfing part learn the rest of it very quickly.

I have two goals for this chapter:

- If you're not hooked up to the Web yet, I want you up and running as quickly and painlessly as possible.

- If you're already navigating the Internet, you'd probably like to understand what is going on inside your computer to make it all happen. I want to demystify the alphabet soup of Open Transport, PPP, TCP, Kbps, and EIEIO (just kidding about the EIEIO part).

First Things First

What is the Web Anyway?

The *World Wide Web* is really just a part of the larger global computer network called the *Internet*. Many people incorrectly use the two terms "Web" and "Internet" interchangeably.

Among my coworkers, I'm a relative newcomer as far as "surfing" the Web is concerned. I didn't get started until mid-1995. Frankly, I put off getting Internet access for two reasons:

- I avoid anything that's **incredibly hyped** in the mainstream press (can you say "Macarena"?).
- I was waiting for it to **get easy.**

It turns out I shouldn't have waited. The hype is terrible, but unlike CB radios and dance crazes, the Web is incredibly useful. And, after a year-and-a-half of waiting, it's still absurdly complicated.

What is the Web good for?

Simple. Three big things: **Getting answers, getting software,** and **communicating.**

Answers: If you want to know how much your car is worth or when your favorite band is going on tour, you can find out. Need to find a phone number? Access the White Pages for the entire United States. Having problems with your computer? Answers abound.

Software: Need an update to your System software? Download it. Interested in a new program? You can often go to the software company's Web site and buy it right there.

Communicating: Want to let someone know you are thinking of them? Send e-mail. Want to find a support group for your special interest or problem? Join a newsgroup or mailing list.

Yes, you can also play games, chat, and look at pictures. If that's what you're into, great. You can use the Web as a recreational diversion, but you'll have a hard time talking your boss into paying for your Internet connection.

It's not easy?

Once you're up and running, it's easy. The problem is getting up and running. That's what this chapter is all about: getting to the heart of what you need to do to get an Internet connection—and understanding how it works—without killing yourself.

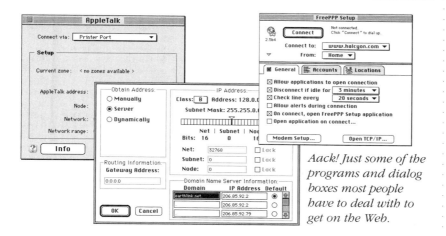

Aack! Just some of the programs and dialog boxes most people have to deal with to get on the Web.

Important Things NOT to Know:

After attending many seminars, as well as reading several big books and dozens of magazine articles over the years, I've learned something the hard way—you can set up and effectively access the World Wide Web **without** knowing any of the following:

- You don't need to know where the Internet came from.
- You don't need to know where it's going.
- You don't need to know how to make a Web page.
- You don't need to know what Fetch, Telnet, FTP, Archie, Anarchie, Gopher, ARPA, DARPA, CERN, CGI, UNIX, IRC, Java, JavaScript, or NIC mean.

For some reason, people think you need to understand this stuff to use the Web. You don't. Millions of people effectively access the Internet everyday *without having any idea* what those things are all about. So relax. We're only going to talk about what is going to help you get surfing.

If you want to know everything . . .

Get your hands on the book *Internet Starter Kit for Macintosh,* by Adam Engst. This is the best book available for Mac users who want to gain a complete understanding of what the Internet is all about. Not only does it talk about Web surfing, but it also has complete chapters on e-mail, discussion groups, and troubleshooting.

It also comes with a terrific CD that includes everything you need to get set up with a service provider and get an online account.

What is Important to Know?

- You need to know what **modem** to use.
- You need to know how to get your Mac to speak the **language** of the Internet.
- You need to know what a **Web browser** is and how it works.
- You need to know how to get an **Internet account** that lets you access the Web.
- You need to know about the **software** that dials the modem and makes the connection for you.

AOL: Getting to the Web the Easy Way

If you want to start surfing with as little hassle as possible, get your hands on an **America Online disk** and sign on. Unless you've been living in a cave for the past few years, you probably already have a pile of these disks sitting on your desk. AOL (America Online) has been stuffing access disks into magazines and sending them in the mail to anyone with a pulse and a mailbox for several years now. Heck, on a United Airlines flight recently, I even got an AOL disk in my bag of pretzels! I used to grumble every time one of these fell out of a magazine, but after remembering that a floppy goes for around a dollar these days, I now say, "Alright! AOL just sent me another buck!" If by some chance you don't have an AOL disk, call 888-265-8002, and they'll send you one.

Here's the deal. AOL is a "proprietary service." This means that when you sign on, you're hooked up to their computers sitting in a big building somewhere in Virginia. Normally your Mac just wanders around inside those giant computers looking at only what they have to offer. It's sort of like being in Disney World—safe, clean, easy, and limited. Heck, you can even wait in line sometimes!

Starting in 1994, AOL allowed you to "break out" of their system and get onto the Internet—a vast, uncontrolled, chaotic, and virtually unlimited environment.

Here's how to do it:

1. **Get a modem.** You want a speedy one—that means one rated at speeds of **28.8 Kbps** (28,800 bits per second). Many Macs come with a modem rate of 14.4 Kbps, which is adequate for Web access, but barely. Prices for 28.8 modems run about $120 to $300 these days.

   Also, get one made by a manufacturer that is fairly well-known and respected. Two popular choices are modems made by Global Village and Supra. Global Village modems tend to be the preferred choice of the Mac geeks I know.

   I avoid lesser-known modem brands because the configuration software you use to get online with AOL, CompuServe, etc., tends to recognize and install the correct software much more easily with a popular modem type.

2. **Get an AOL account.** Double-click the installer program on the floppy. The software will ask you a number of straightforward questions, and within fifteen minutes you'll be hooked up and roaming around inside their computers in Virginia.

America Online version 3.0 just became available for Power Mac users. It's on a CD and includes a browser.

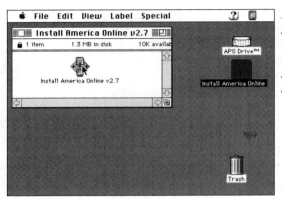

Double-click the AOL install disk. The software will walk you through setting up an AOL account.

3. **Download the AOL Web Browser installer.** If you installed AOL's software from a floppy disk, you haven't yet received their Internet access software.

Just type **Command K,** then type in the word "upgrade." This will take you to a screen where you can download AOL's Web access (browser) software installer.

After you download this stuff, **quit** AOL.

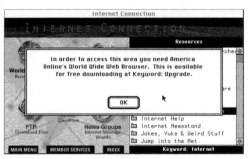

Installing AOL isn't enough to access the Web. You must also get their browser and TCP software.

4. **Install the browser.** Double-click on the "Install AOL Browser" program, and it will put everything you need in the right place. The two main things it installs are the program **Web Browser** and the program **TCPack for AOL** (System software so your Mac can talk TCP/IP, the language of the Internet).

5. **Log back on to AOL.** In the Main Menu you'll find the "Internet Connection" button. Click on it, and your Web browser software will immediately launch. In a minute you'll be on the Web!

TCP/IP stands for Transmission Control Protocol/Internet Protocol, but no one will ever expect you to know that.

After you install the AOL browser and TCPack for AOL, click the "Internet Connection" button to get on the Web.

You will then be able to type into the "Current URL" edit box a URL (Uniform Resource Locator, or Web address) that can take you to someone's Web page. (More about URLs later in this chapter.)

Type a Web address in the "Current URL" box in AOL's browser to surf the Internet.

Why AOL's Web Access is Neat

- **It's easy.** It took me less than an hour from the moment I first popped in the AOL install disk to browsing real live Web pages. (That includes time spent upgrading my buggy System software.) If everything goes well, which it usually does, you could be up and running in twenty minutes.

- **You can set up your own Web site.** AOL lets you establish a site with your very own Web pages (up to several megabytes of information and graphics) that other people can view.

- **You can dial-in from practically anywhere.** America Online has local access numbers all over the U.S. and Europe. In addition, they have an 800 number ($6 an hour) you can use.

Why AOL's Web Access is Not-so-Neat

- **AOL can be slow.** Since America Online is so popular, their computers can get clogged with people logging in. This sometimes brings things to a crawl. In addition, some cities have access lines that are 14.4 Kbps or slower. I took a vacation to Hawaii last year, and the fastest local line I could get to AOL was a glacial 2400 baud (2.4 Kbps).

- **AOL can be unreliable.** As AOL dedicates much of their resources to expanding membership rather than improving the system, it sometimes "goes down." It went down for nineteen hours a while ago, just at a time when I desperately needed to send a file to a client. Once or twice a week I can count on not being able to get in for some reason. Just today, it took me ten minutes of repeated attempts to get in. As you can tell, I'm starting to get a bit peeved about it.

Note!

With AOL version 3.0, **you can use any installed browser.** *Simply log on to AOL, then open your browser of choice.*

- **AOL's browser is nonstandard.** People creating Web pages generally assume the viewer will be using Netscape Navigator or Microsoft Internet Explorer to look at their pages. AOL's browser doesn't have all the features of those programs, so it can't "see" all the cool things people might put on their pages. In some cases, a page can confuse the AOL browser and make it crash.

  Version 3.0 of America Online uses a version of Microsoft Internet Explorer. This should help make Web browsing through America Online more standard and stable.

ISPs: Getting to the Web the "Real" Way

Most folks accessing the Web are not doing it through AOL. Instead, they have established a connection using some other (usually local) company or organization called an **Internet Service Provider,** or **ISP** for short. There are literally thousands of these companies across the country that can act as an "on ramp" for you to get to the Internet.

Before we get into the nitty-gritty of using one of these companies, let me suggest a simplified version of how you *should* be able to get on the Web.

How it SHOULD Work

If I were in charge, here's how it would go:

1. Buy a modem—plug it in.
2. Buy the browsing software—install it.
3. Type an access phone number and a credit card number into the Web browser.
4. Double-click the Web browser to connect to the Internet.
5. Get a bill every month; pay it.

Why it's Not that Easy

Here are the main roadblocks to this utopian scenario:

Problem: Macintoshes (and PCs as well) were never designed to talk the "language" of the Internet. This language is called **TCP/IP.** Your System software needs to be enhanced for this to happen.

Solution: Apple has two Control Panels that can make your Mac talk the Internet talk. One is called **TCP/IP** (TCP/IP comes with newer Macs and works with Apple's **Open Transport**). Another is called **MacTCP** (for use with older Macs and older System software.) You must have Open Transport's TCP/IP Control Panel **or** MacTCP installed to connect to the Internet.

Problem: For some weird reason, Web browser programs can't make the initial connection to the Internet all by themselves. Once again, a System-modifying Extension must do it.

Solution: A nonprofit group has supplied Mac users with a program called **FreePPP.** Its job is to dial the phone and tell the computer at the other end who you are and why it's okay to let you in.

Open Transport is Apple's low-level networking architecture now. It is composed of a number of pieces of code, of which the TCP/IP Control Panel is one part.

Okay—So How Do I Get Connected with an ISP?

Following are the seven basic steps to get you up and running with an ISP and a direct connection to the Internet

1. **Get a modem.** As previously described, get a popular model rated at speeds of at least 14.4 Kbps. **A speed of 28.8 Kbps is much better.**

2. **Find a Good ISP.** Here's how an ISP works:

   Odds are that somewhere in your town there is at least one company that has a high-speed data line called a **T1** (or maybe a **T3**) line. This is a very expensive cable that is much faster and larger than a normal phone line. Imagine that a phone line is a straw; a T1 line is like a firehose.

   ISPs also have a bunch of special computers hooked up to a bunch of modems and telephone lines.

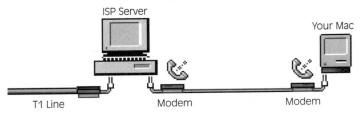

The Internet Service Provider connects to the Web with a high-speed line that supports many users.

   Does an ISP have to be local? Nope. All kinds of big national companies are getting into the act. AT&T, EarthLink, CompuServe, and many others are offering Internet access. National companies offer 800 numbers for access (for which you are charged $4 to $12 per hour). Frequent travelers like this a lot. When you get an account with a national provider, they let you dial into their computers (through a normal phone line) and hookup to their high-speed Internet connection. (I prefer local providers because it's often easier to get the Mac expertise I need.)

Ask around, and find out who provides the best connection service in town. **Talking to folks at a Mac user group** meeting is a good way to get this kind of information. (In Chapter Thirteen I describe how to find a user group in your area.) Here's what you want to find out:

Who specializes in Macintosh? Not all ISPs are Mac-focused. Find one who can intelligently answer your questions and is used to working with your hardware. It's very important that the provider give you clear instructions on how to configure your Mac. See if they'll fax you documentation on how to set your software.

How is their capacity? Try calling their access number at busy access times like high noon or 7 P.M. If you get a consistent busy signal, consider using another provider. Ask around. Talk to people who use this provider and ask if they notice frequent slowdowns or busy signals.

What are their prices? Prices range from $15 to $30 a month for general "unlimited" Internet access. It can be cheaper to go with a provider who has some access limitations, like limiting you to two hours maximum at one sitting.

Shop for and choose a provider without leaving your desk!

Both the *Internet Starter Kit for Macintosh* ($35) and the *Apple Internet Connection Kit* ($99) come with a special CD-ROM database. Tell the database where you live, and it will tell you what Internet access providers have service to your area.

These all-in-one packages also include Web browsing software.

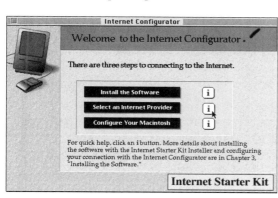

With the Internet Starter Kit for Macintosh *you can click on a provider, and the database will install and* **configure** *all your Internet software for you automatically.*

3. **Install the Web browser.** Perhaps the most important piece of software you need is the Web browser. Some common browsing programs include:

   - **Netscape Navigator** (most people use this Web browser)
   - **Microsoft Internet Explorer** (fewer users, but getting more popular)
   - **Cyberdog** (gaining popularity)
   - **Mosaic** (not so many users anymore; is no longer officially being developed)

You absolutely must have one of these programs to get going. I recommend you get Netscape Navigator or Microsoft Internet Explorer. You can find Netscape for sale at a computer store or mail-order outlet. In many cases, when you sign up with a service provider they will send you a disk with one of these Web browsers on it.

Also, you can download Internet Explorer or Netscape from their Web sites at microsoft.com or netscape.com. But how can you go to their Web sites if you don't have a browser? Many people initially get a copy of the software from a friend and then "officially" **register it** at the Netscape or Microsoft home page. Internet Explorer is free; Netscape is free to download, but then you must register and send in your small fee.

4. **Configure the FreePPP part.** Okay. Now it starts getting "techie." You have to let your Mac know about the call it's going to make to your service provider.

   FreePPP will dial the phone for you and make the initial connection. PPP stands for **Point-to-Point Protocol.** Some providers use an ancestor of PPP called **SLIP** (Serial Line Internet Protocol) to act as the phone dialer and information providing software. If you have a choice, use PPP. It's faster and more reliable.

   After making sure that the FreePPP Extension is in your Extensions folder, launch the program **FreePPP Setup.** FreePPP Setup tells the FreePPP Extension what phone number(s) to dial and other details described below.

Once again, **your ISP will tell you** what numbers to type in. Here are the kinds of things you need to do:

- **Create an Account:** Click the **Account** tab and then the **Edit** button. Enter the name of your provider, the phone number they tell you to use, your user name, and your password.

- **Set the Connection:** Click on the **Connection** tab, and set the port speed. Notice how high mine is set (57,600 bps—my modem is 28,800 bps). **Always set the port speed at a higher connection speed than your modem can run.** Heck—I've been driving at 55 (okay, 65) on roads capable of 85 for years!

- **Set the Flow Control.** Your provider will tell you how to set it. Flow Control allows you to set "handshaking" options for how your Mac and the computer at your ISP communicate. As a general rule, the "CTS Only" option will work best for most people. If "CTS Only" doesn't work, "CTS & RTS (DTR)" is the next best choice. If you have a PowerBook Duo or 500 series with an internal modem, the "None" option may work better.

- **Options.** Most people can ignore the contents of the Options part of this setup.

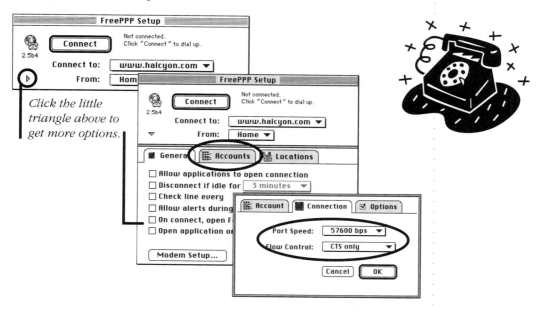

Click the little triangle above to get more options.

5. **Configure the TCP/IP Part.** Open the TCP/IP Control Panel. Now, you have to tell your TCP software about the **Domain Name Server Address** (also called the **DNS** address). These numbers will be supplied to you by your ISP. All you have to do is type the numbers into the TCP/IP Control Panel.

These numbers signify your server's "identity" on the Internet. If you forget to enter them, you won't be able to get anywhere online. Think of these numbers as Directory Assistance: your Mac will call these numbers to find out where in the world a certain Web page is. For example—when you enter "www.apple.com" into your Web browser, your Mac asks the Domain Name Server where that site is located. The DNS responds with Apple's "IP" number, and you're on your way.

In the example below, I have entered the numbers for my local provider in Seattle, which only work with that provider. Your numbers will be different.

Set the "Connect via" pop-up menu to "FreePPP."

Set the "Configure" pop-up menu to "Using PPP Server."

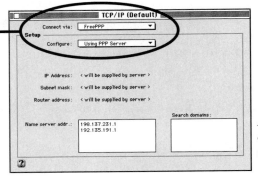

Here's where you enter the DNS numbers.

In MacTCP, click the PPP icon, then click the "More…" button.

In this dialog box, click the "Server" radio button.

What if you don't have the TCP/IP Control Panel? No problem. Odds are you are using a Mac that's configured with the older Control Panel **MacTCP.**

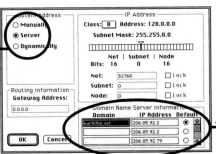

You can enter the DNS address, as shown here.

On the left side, the second and third fields should contain periods only. On the right side, the first two fields should be the same.

6. **Now restart your computer!** It's always a good idea to reboot after configuring these Controls Panels.

7. **Log in.** Tell FreePPP setup to dial the phone for you. All you have to do is **click the Connect button!**

   If all goes well, you'll hear FreePPP dial the phone, and then you'll hear some weird modem noises. When the "Connect" button becomes a "Disconnect" button, you're logged on!

8. **Start Surfing!** The only thing left to do is to **launch your Web browser.** Just double-click the Web browser program and it will automatically take you to a Web page somewhere. The default page it automatically brings up is called "Home." You can set your Web browser's preferences to make Home any page on the Internet you want, such as your own home page, a search engine page, or your favorite Web site.

   Usually, Home is preset to take you to your service provider's page, or maybe to the company that made the Web browser's page. Feel free to change it to a more appropriate page, using the browser preferences. All you have to do is copy the URL from the URL location box of the page you want and paste it into your Preferences dialog box. Or if you know the address by heart or have it written down somewhere, just type it in.

Once your favorite page is set as Home, click the Home button in Netscape to take you right to that page.

In Netscape, you'll find the Preferences in the Options menu.

Other Tidbits

Here are a few other tidbits of information about the Web.

Getting Around

To go to a certain Web page, just type in the address or **URL** (Uniform Resource Locator) into the **Location** (or **Address**) field of the Web browser, then hit Return.

You don't have to type the **http://** part of the address. Your Web browser already knows that part. For example, instead of typing http: //www.thunderlizard.com to go the Thunder Lizard home page, just type **www. thunderlizard.com.** That is the **domain name.**

In Netscape and Internet Explorer 3.0 (Mac only) all you need to type is **thunderlizard,** and the browser will figure out the rest.

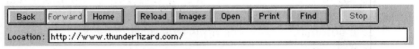

Type the URL into the Location field, then hit Return. Your browser will add the http://.

What is a URL?

If you're confused by all the weird syntax you need to type to bring up a Web page, you're not alone. Take a URL like:

http://www.apple.com

What does all that gobbledygook mean?

The **http://** part means you want to access a World Wide Web page. Web pages are transferred with the **h**yper**t**ext **t**ransfer **p**rotocol. This all means it's something designed to be seen by a browser, as opposed to a prefix of "news://" or "ftp://," which looks for something else. In most browsers you don't have to type in the http:// part.

The **www** part does not appear in all Web addresses. It stands for World Wide Web, of course, but it is more of a convention than a required part of an address.

The **.com** part means that this is a site held at a **commercial** location versus a school (**.edu**) or a non-profit (**.org**).

Okay, none of this is all that crucial. Here's something that is important: Let's say you are looking at a page on the Web that has a link you can click. Maybe it says "Click here for some free games." You click on it. Sure enough, it takes you to a neat free games page on the Apple site. You look in the URL location box (shown on the previous page) and see the address:

http://www.apple.com/freesoftware/games/

(By the way, this is not a real site—I just made it up.)

If you read that URL backwards, it says you're inside the **games** folder, which is inside the **freesoftware** folder, which is at the **Apple** Web site. If you delete the "games" part of the URL and hit Return, you will move up a level in the directory structure to the "free software" area and probably be able to access other interesting (free stuff) pages!

Those Dang .HQX Files!

Okay, so by this point you may have already gone out and downloaded a file. You went to a games page, clicked on a special link, and sure enough, it started copying a file to your hard disk. But wait! You thought you had asked for the game Asteroids, but instead you got some weird file called "aster-111.hqx."

map.hqx

A blank, generic icon with an extension of .hqx is a binhexed file.

To make things worse, when you double-click on it, nothing happens! What the heck is going on?

You did download Asteroids, but it's been **"binhexed."** Binhex is just a confusing term for a special type of packaging that protects the file. Think of the file as having a protective covering that needs to be removed. (By the way, if you want to sound like a real Web expert, just throw the word "binhex" into a conversation sometime.)

Okay, so how do you extract the file out of the binhex packaging? Easy, get your hands on the program **StuffIt Expander.** It's freeware, so you don't even have to pay for it. In fact, it's included with Netscape 3.0. If you have StuffIt Expander on your hard disk, files will be **automatically uncompressed** when they're downloaded—it's great.

StuffIt Expander

StuffIt Expander is an indispensable utility. Get it.

The only problem with getting a free copy of StuffIt Expander by downloading it from the Web is that StuffIt Expander will be **binhexed!** Doh! That means you'll have to uncompress it before you can use it! Instead of downloading it, try getting a copy from a friend or your local Mac user group.

After you have uncompressed the binhexed file, you will have another file that is the real thing. You can throw away the .hqx version.

Creating bookmarks

Netscape calls them "Bookmarks," and Explorer calls them "Favorites." I don't care what you call them—just make sure you use them!

When you're at a page you really like, add it to your bookmarks or favorites list. This way you'll be able to come back any time you want without having to type in the URL.

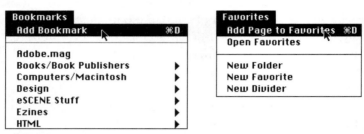

Use Bookmarks or Favorites to keep great sites handy.

In the Favorites menu of Explorer, as shown above, you can easily see that you can make new folders and dividers to organize your favorites. You actually have more options of things to do with your bookmarks in Netscape than in Explorer, but in Netscape you must first open the Bookmarks Window from the Window menu. Once that window is open, there is a new menu called "Item." Use it to create folders and dividers to organize your bookmarks. Everything in the Bookmarks Window is drag-and-drop, so file away.

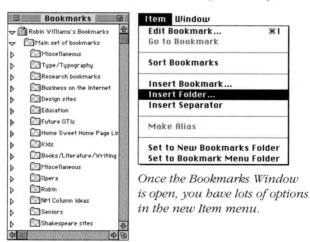

Once the Bookmarks Window is open, you have lots of options in the new Item menu.

Search Engines and Directories

What's the most important page on the Web? The one that lets you **find** other pages of course! There are search engines and directories created specifically to find information on the Internet.

A **search engine** is an index of information created and updated automatically by programs (called robots or spiders). Use a search engine when you want to find a specific piece of information that probably would not have an entire Web site devoted to it, such as "What was the name of the hotel that burned in a fire after an earthquake on March 23, 1957, on Market Street in San Francisco?" **AltaVista** is one of the best search engines.

A **directory,** or **catalog,** is an index of information that has been created and organized by humans. A directory helps you find entire Web sites that are devoted to specific topics. Use a directory when you have a broad topic in mind, such as Shakespeare or woodworking. The most popular directory is **Yahoo!,** located at www.yahoo.com.

My favorite search engine is Digital's **AltaVista** at www.altavista.digital.com.

Robin's current favorite search engine is **Excite** at www.excite.com.

By entering search requests or by burrowing through category listings, you can prune through millions of Web pages to find ones on just the topic(s) you want.

In Chapter Thirteen I'll show you some Mac-related Web pages that can help you find the answers you need.

For More Info

I strongly recommend the Visual QuickStart books on Netscape and Internet Explorer from Peachpit Press (www.peachpit.com). You will learn amazing things from these books, and they're small with lots of pictures so it's painless. You'll be surprised at what you don't know.

Important Things to Remember

- You can get on the Web very quickly and easily through America Online.

- Getting an independent Internet Service Provider (ISP) is usually cheaper and better in the long term.

- A Web browser such as Netscape Navigator or Microsoft Internet Explorer lets you view pages and navigate from one page to another.

- The TCP/IP or MacTCP Control Panels let your Mac speak the same language all the other computers on the Internet speak.

- FreePPP dials the phone and sets up the connection to the Web.

- Get a copy of StuffIt Expander so you can uncompress the files you download.

- Bookmark your favorite sites on the Web, and organize your bookmarks so they are easy to use.

- Learn to use the search engines and directories to find the Web sites you need.

Stay on Top of It   13

Know Your Resources

Keeping up with the ever-changing Mac arena is a real challenge. Knowing what to buy (and what not to buy), taking advantage of the hidden features of your software, getting great deals, and making sure you're using the best software for your needs can be a full-time job.

Given the limited time at your disposal, how can you get the most relevant information without spending a ton of time and money?

Here are the resources the experts use to stay current.

Periodicals and Magazines

Although my information gathering is shifting more and more to the online arena, I still get most of my news from magazines. I've been a voracious reader of computer magazines for the past 13 years, and I've got to say that my reading habits have changed dramatically since I started. Although I still read many of the same publications, I now read them much differently—and I encourage you to follow a similar model.

First of all, remember that *just because it's in print doesn't mean it's true!* I have a lot of fun going through old magazines and seeing predictions and analyses that were proven way wrong by time. One famous (and still prolific) writer claimed in 1984 that the mouse was ridiculous and would never gain popularity. Many still-popular writers fell for the "Macs will soon be cheaper and faster than Windows machines" propaganda that Apple spewed in 1991, and they wrote articles following that theme.

Programs you've never heard of or never actually use, like Lotus Jazz, Filevision, and HyperCard, were all given press worthy of the second coming. Pundits claimed they would forever change how we would all use our computers. Once again, totally incorrect. (Okay, HyperCard was revolutionary, and many multimedia developers still use it, but it was supposed to become the programming tool for *everyone.*)

Reviews frequently contain inaccuracies or are just plain wrong about important details. Software programs are so complicated these days that it's almost impossible to know everything about a piece of software.

One way to help insure you're getting the straight story is to start noticing **who** wrote the article. Soon you'll be able to avoid writers who are consistently off base, while targeting those who really know their stuff.

Here are a few Mac-centric writers who are consistently on target:

Ric Ford	Bob LeVitus	Jim Heid
Cary Lu	Deke McClelland	David Pogue
Lon Poole	Joseph Schorr	Adam Engst

Okay. So now you have some idea **who** to read. Even more important is **what** to read. Here are the magazines and periodicals that the experts rely on to stay informed.

Macworld

If I had to pick just one Mac-centric magazine to subscribe to, it would be *Macworld*. The editors go to great lengths to provide Mac professionals with articles that are timely, relevant, objective, and complete. Two of the top Mac experts—David Pogue and Joseph Schorr—have monthly columns that are not to be missed.

Macworld is available at newsstands worldwide, $4.95. Find their Web site at www.macworld.com. Call (800) 288-6848 to subscribe.

MacUser

There's lots of good stuff in *MacUser*. The content overlaps significantly with *Macworld,* so you don't really need to get both (although many of us do). Graphics professionals will appreciate the prepress and graphics coverage.

MacUser is also on the newsstands, $3.99. To subscribe, call (415) 478-5600. Or check out www.zdnet.com/macuser/.

MacAddict

MacAddict is the new kid on the block. It takes an in-your-face, anti-Windows approach that has started to become the fashion among a few myopic Mac publications. Despite its incredibly high price ($7.99!), it's a good read for new users, and the issues I reviewed included a useful CD of shareware and utilities (mostly stuff easily downloaded off the Web, CompuServe, or AOL). It's available at newsstands.

Call (415) 468-4869, or check out www.macaddict.com.

MacWEEK

MacWEEK is one for the Mac fanatic. A ton of industry coverage—who's buying whom, who had a bad quarter, and whose products are buggy or recalled. Some of the opinion columnists (like Ric Ford and Adam Engst) offer great insights, while a select few of the long-time columnists tend to be clueless.

Fill out the application/subscription card, and the publication is free *if you qualify*. The problem is, they're really picky. It seems that if you're not a purchasing director for a big company, they're not interested in giving you a free subscription. In that case, you must pay $125 a year.

I must admit that I don't know anyone who actually pays for *MacWEEK*. I also don't know anyone who actually qualifies either. Despite this,

I know a ton of people who get it. Let's just put it this way—some folks stretch the truth a bit when they fill out that excessive subscription form.

Call (609) 796-8230 for subscription info, or aim your browser at their Web site at www.macweek.com.

Digital Chicago

This used to be called *Mac Chicago* before they began pandering to the Windows users (just kidding—it's still 90 percent Mac content). If you're a design professional or someone who produces multimedia or Web content, you'll want this publication that is consistently packed with good stuff. If you want in-depth coverage of QuarkXPress, Photoshop, PageMaker, Illustrator, and FreeHand, this is a great read.

You can call (847) 439-6575 for subscription info, or find them at www.digitalchi.com.

Publish

If you can endure the constant letters to the editor complaining there's "too much Mac coverage!" right next to letters claiming there's "too much Windows coverage!," *Publish* will give you a lot of good information about graphics and publishing. I'd say it's a must-have for the serious Mac-graphics geek.

Call (800) 656-7495 for a subscription, $4.95 an issue, or check out their Web site at www.publish.com.

Adobe Magazine

Adobe Magazine is the best desktop publishing magazine around—even considering you won't find anything about QuarkXPress or FreeHand in it. If you use Photoshop, Illustrator, Acrobat, Premiere, and/or PageMaker though, get ready for tons of interesting tips, tricks, and techniques.

One of the best things about *Adobe Magazine* is that it's free to anyone in the U.S. or Canada owning an Adobe product. Call (206) 628-2321 for subscription info. You can also visit www.adobemag.com.

BMUG Journal

Although some of the articles focus on niche Mac usage (see the User Groups section below), this twice-a-year, 400-page publication contains some of the hottest techniques and insights available. Their no-punches-pulled approach to reviewing software is a breath of fresh air. Call (510) 549-2684.

User Groups

In terms of getting your money's worth, nothing beats joining a good Mac User Group, affectionately called a MUG. In every large city world-wide (and in many smaller cities), you'll find at least one of these clubs dedicated to dispensing Mac-related information and techniques. For anywhere between $20 to $50 you'll get a year-long membership, which entitles you to attend the main meeting as well as the SIG (Special Interest Group) meetings. SIGs cover specific topics ranging from using word processors to 3D modeling. Robin runs a Beginners' SIG at the Santa Fe Mac User Group each month.

Meetings usually have presentations that cover things like tips and tricks, how to speed up your system, new bugs that have been discovered and how to get around them, and lots more. Advanced users get to share techniques, beginners pick up useful tidbits, and everyone gets their questions answered.

At the general meetings for the entire membership, vendors often make appearances to show off their latest hardware and software offerings. In addition, many vendors will offer member discounts on purchases of their products.

Another benefit to joining a user group can be the newsletters they publish. Almost every one of these organizations publishes a monthly, quarterly, or annual newsletter with Macintosh tips. My favorite is the *BMUG Journal.* I joined this Berkeley-based user group many years ago and have yet to attend a meeting. I pay my annual dues ($55) just to get the 400-page "newsletter" they publish twice a year. Their "Choice Products" section is *the* place to see which hardware, software, and service companies are taking great care of their Mac users.

The *BMUG Journal* also occasionally scoops the big magazines — like when they showed how most Mac IIsi owners could speed up their machines 20 percent for around ten dollars. This "clock-chipping" procedure was soon covered by the big guys like *Macworld* and *MacUser*. Their irreverent (and totally accurate) review of Microsoft Word 6.0, "Pass the Cranberry Sauce—This One's a Real Turkey," received national attention in the *New York Times*, and acted as the catalyst for a general uproar in the Mac community concerning Microsoft's interface negligence.

Unfortunately, you'll also have to wade through a few self-indulgent "lifestyle" articles (like the obligatory how-I-went-to-the-computer-store-in-1987-and-bought-a-Mac-and-my-life-has-totally-changed article). Overall though, the *BMUG Journal* is Number One on many people's lists for getting great Mac info. BMUG can be reached at (510) 549-2684.

Where to find a user group near you

To find out what groups are available in your area (or any area you plan to visit), call Apple's User Group Connection at (800) 538-9696 and they can clue you in. They'll ask you for the zip code of the area in which you want to find a group, and they'll give you the contact person's name and phone number.

Online Resources

There's no better place to receive timely Mac info than through an online source. With a modem, a phone line, and the right software, you can access a vast library of technical data, support, and software.

More and more Web sites crop up everyday that focus on all types of hardware- and software-related issues. When I'm confronted with a technical problem, I head for a Web site before I reach for a book or magazine.

While commercial online services (America Online, CompuServe, etc.) are good places to get much of this information, the Internet is better. Luckily, America Online and CompuServe make it easy to get Internet access from their software.

Okay, what the heck can we do online that's so great? Here's a list of useful things you can do and which online services offer them.

Getting Software

You can get almost any type of software online. Whether you're looking for an arcade game or some new word processing software, odds are you can download just what you need.

Although major applications like Photoshop and Word aren't for sale on the Web yet (a minimal version of Photoshop would take six hours for a typical user to download), we'll see that kind of thing just as soon as we get faster phone or cable lines in place.

Internet

By far, the Internet offers the most software for download. All the major vendors have Web pages, and many sites have public domain software (programs that can be legally and freely distributed) for you to access.

If it's commercial software or upgrades you're after, use your browser and type the vendor's name in the **Open Location** dialog box. In Netscape Navigator or Internet Explorer, it's this easy:

1. Press **Command L**
2. Type **Adobe**
3. Hit **Return**

Next thing you know, you're there! The vendor's home page usually makes it clear where to go to get the software you want.

The Command L keyboard shortcut in both Netscape and Internet Explorer lets you type in a destination easily.

Freeware, shareware, and public domain software

Online there are several major libraries of public domain software. The most famous is the **Info-Mac Archive.** To check out over two gigabytes of freeware and shareware that you can download, steer your browser toward ftp://mirror.apple.com/mirrors/Info-Mac.Archive. Be sure to capitalize the address exactly as you see here.

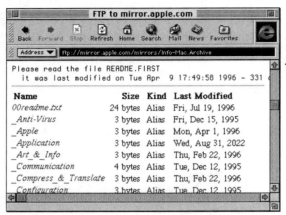

The Info-Mac Archive has more great Mac software available for download than anywhere else.

Shareware.com

Shareware.com is another rich source of downloadable software. Just type **shareware** in the location box of your browser and you will arrive. Use the menus and edit boxes to search.

America Online

All of the major software companies maintain a presence on America Online. Press Command K to bring up the **Go to Keyword** dialog box. Just enter the name of the company and click OK. If that doesn't work, try typing the product name.

All of the major software companies provide information about their products on AOL.

You can also search AOL's huge collection of public domain software. From the Go To menu, choose "Search Software Libraries."

Tech Support Databases

Apple, Microsoft, Adobe, and many other companies have database locations you can access that contain documents created by their tech support people. Often these databases are searchable, and their documents can provide answers to problems.

Web-based databases

The "big four" sites that Macintosh users will want to access for trouble-shooting support are:

- **Apple**   www.apple.com
- **Microsoft**   www.microsoft.com
- **Adobe**   www.adobe.com
- **Claris**   www.claris.com

Each of these sites contains tech support databases that you can search by keyword.

Go straight to the source—Apple's Web site lets you search for answers.

Other great Web resources

Besides the sites maintained by the big guys, there are several smaller sites that are treasure troves of technical help.

Ted Landau's **MacFixIt** page at **www.macfixit.com** is a terrific spot. Ted works night and day to stay on top of problems that Mac users are experiencing with their hardware and system software. This is one of the sites I check daily.

The **Complete Conflict Compendium** at **www.quillserv.com/www/c3/c3.html** lists Mac programs that don't get along, discusses the symptoms they manifest, and offers suggestions on how to solve the problem.

Another terrific site to check daily is Ric Ford's **MacinTouch** site at **www.macintouch.com**. It's a great place to find super-current information on pressing Apple software updates and glitches. This site also discusses all the important issues facing Mac professionals today, and it profiles interesting new programs.

Searching America Online and CompuServe for tech support

Searchable vendor databases are harder to find on the commercial services such as America Online or CompuServe. It seems more and more of these resources are moving onto the Internet. For example, if you try to use Microsoft's tech support database on AOL, it sends you out to the Web to Microsoft's home page!

Join Discussion Groups and Forums

Internet

The Internet has discussion groups, called *newsgroups,* that can make getting answers easy. Just about every software- or hardware-related issue has a group dedicated to it. Need to know why QuarkXPress crashes every time you start it up? Check in on a Quark newsgroup and scan the previous postings—often someone else has had the same problem and has posted a question about it. You can either scroll down and look for a response that gave a solution, or maybe e-mail the originator and ask how they fixed things.

Can't find anyone else with the same problem? Post your own message, and check in later for a response. It's not uncommon to receive a message from a software company tech support guru, and you never have to wait on hold!

How do you find these newsgroups? One way is to go to a Web page that contains links to them. One popular place to go is the **Well Connected Mac** site at **www.macfaq.com/newsgroups.html** .

Another easy way to find a specific group is to go a search engine that searches newsgroup postings, such as DejaNews at **www. dejanews.com**. Enter a search request that includes a word or two of your problem or need. You'll probably come up with several matches that take you straight to where the discussions are going on.

Before you post a message to a news-group, read their FAQ (frequently asked questions) file. If it is a common question, the answer will be in the FAQ. Members of news-groups get very annoyed with newcomers who jump into discussions and post messages without having read the FAQ. The general rule is to hang around, listen to what's going on, and see how things are done in a newsgroup before you chime in.

Need an answer? Odds are someone else has asked the same question before—check a newsgroup!

America Online

AOL is known for its extensive number of forums for discussing software. Every major (and many minor) program has a discussion group dedicated to it. These postings are *threaded,* which means that a message will have the response(s) attached to it. Frequently you'll find a bunch of responses (and responses to responses) that give many possible solutions to the problem in question.

From AOL's Main Menu, just click on the "Computing" icon, and you can choose which software or hardware category you want to discuss.

AOL has lots of places to talk about hardware and software with other users.

CompuServe

CompuServe is known for having the largest number of discussion groups of all the online services.

To access CompuServe's forums, just use the "Go Forums" command.

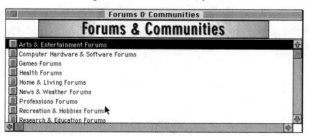

CompuServe is known for having the most in-depth computing discussion groups.

Get on a Mailing List

If you have an e-mail address, you can get free publications sent to you electronically on a regular basis (usually weekly). These publications cover the latest developments, bug warnings, and discussions about the use of your Macintosh or favorite software.

Getting these mailings is easy. All you have to do is send a message to a special address, and you're automatically on the list. For example, one of the most popular (150,000 subscribers) and useful Internet newsletters is called **TidBITS.** It focuses on Macintosh and Internet-related subjects. To get this every week, all I had to do was send an e-mail message to this address: **tidbits-on@tidbits.com**. The message read: "subscribe tidbits Steve Broback." You can do the same thing (substitute your name, and don't type the period at the end), and every Tuesday you'll magically receive a 32K text file covering very cool stuff.

An even easier way to subscribe to this and other valuable lists is to go to the **Well Connected Mac** site at **www.macfaq.com/mailing lists.html** and check out their "list of lists." There you can peruse the lists and publications available and fill out a simple form so you can receive the online publications you want.

Access Periodicals and Article Archives

Many print (as well as electronic) publications archive their articles and reviews online. Here are some sites that have a wealth of previously published editorial material surrounding Mac usage. All the material is available for download.

Macworld	www.macworld.com
TidBITS	www.tidbits.com
MacinTouch	www.macintouch.com
Apple	www.apple.com
MacUser	www.zdnet.com/macuser/
MacWEEK	www.macweek.com/

*An extremely important part of getting **on** a list is knowing how to get **off** the list. When you subscribe, you will receive instructions on how to unsubscribe when you need to. **Save those instructions.** If you ever decide you don't want to be on the mailing list anymore, you cannot simply send a message to the mailing list. If you do, thousands of people will hate you because your message goes to everyone on the list, none of whom can take you off the list. **Save those unsubscribing instructions!***

Books

Of the hundreds of available Mac-centric titles, here are a few of the top choices for making you a master of the ever-changing Mac world.

The Macintosh Bible, by the "Dirty Dozen," Peachpit Press

The "Dirty Dozen" are some of the biggest Mac hotshots in the industry. Authors like Ted Alspach, Ted Landau, and Kathleen Tinkel have put together a 991-page tome that discusses a wide-range of subjects. This all-purpose book covers everything from getting on the Internet to how to be a spreadsheet jockey. It's a great book for someone who uses a lot of different programs and wants to get the most out of all of them.

Macworld Mac Secrets, by David Pogue and Joseph Schorr, IDG Books

If you're looking for a big (1,193 pages) Mac book, this is the one. It covers practically everything you could ever want to know about the Mac or its System software. This book has tons of useful tips and techniques, and if you want to know trivia such as when the Mac SE was discontinued or the hidden secrets of the Puzzle desk accessory, this volume has it all.

Sad Macs, Bombs, and Other Disasters, by Ted Landau, Peachpit Press

If your Mac isn't acting right, this book will tell you what's wrong and how to fix it. I consider it an indispensable reference.

Important Things to Remember

- Don't believe everything you read!
- Join a user group.
- When you read an article, note who wrote it— good or bad—so you'll know whom to trust.
- If you can get only one magazine, make it *Macworld.*
- If you want to really stay on top of it all, get a modem and Internet access.
- Get on an Internet mailing list.

Working with PCs and Windows

14

The Best of Both Worlds

Okay, let's face it. Most of the computer users in the world use a different type of computer than we do. We Mac users are sometimes made to feel like outcasts because of this. What most people don't realize is that **Mac users have the best of both worlds.**

Whatever you want to call it—PC-compatibility, Windows-compatibility, being IBM-compatible—it doesn't matter. The Mac can do it—and it's easier than you think.

Even if you plan on using only Mac software and creating exclusively Mac documents, odds are that someone, sometime will give you a disk and/or files from that "other" platform.

Here are some ways to make your Mac fit in a Windows world.

"Instant" Compatibility: Using PC Disks and/or Files on Your Mac

Most Mac users can get all the Windows compatibility they need from Apple's standard hardware and software. They don't need to buy anything extra, install any hardware, or hassle with cables. Here's the scenario that works for most people:

Super Easy Compatibility—Using PC Disks in a Mac

Ninety percent of the time when someone asks me if their Mac is Windows-compatible, they have a simple goal in mind. They want to bring work home.

Most of these folks have a PC running DOS or Windows at the office and a Mac at home. They want to take a project from work home on a floppy and finish it on the Mac. Luckily, Apple has done a great job of making this easy for most people.

First thing to know: **All Macs built since 1988 have a disk drive that can use PC disks**. Mac Plus and Mac II owners are out of luck, as are about half of the Mac SE owners. These early machines have an incompatible type of floppy drive.

Next important tidbit: **You need special software to make this disk drive work with PC disks**. All Macs sold within the past few years come with the program **PC Exchange.** This Control Panel allows PC disks to appear on the Desktop as if they were standard Mac disks. Restart with PC Exchange in your Control Panels Folder and PC disks will work like magic.

DOS Disk

With PC Exchange loaded, this icon will appear on the Desktop when you insert a PC disk.

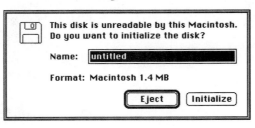

This disk is unreadable by this Macintosh. Do you want to initialize the disk?

Name: untitled

Format: Macintosh 1.4 MB

Eject   Initialize

Without PC Exchange installed, you'll get this message when you insert a PC disk.

Help for Older Macs

If you have an older Mac that doesn't have PC Exchange, you probably have the program **Apple File Exchange** instead. This is a crude, but effective, little program Apple used to provide free with all Macs. Unlike PC Exchange, you have to double-click Apple File Exchange. It brings up a dialog box that will let you insert the PC disk, and then transfer the file(s) over to your hard disk to work on them. **The trick is** you need to open Apple File Exchange *before* you put your disk in.

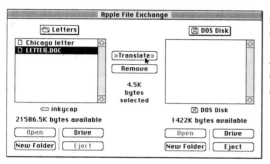

If you don't have PC Exchange, you may have the older utility Apple File Exchange. Here it is copying a file from the hard disk to a PC disk.

Compatible Applications

Now, if you are using Excel, Word, WordPerfect, ClarisWorks, File-Maker, PageMaker, or any other program that has both Mac and PC versions, you'll be happy to know that the file formats are usually identical on both platforms (assuming you are using the same version number on both machines—Word 5 may have trouble with Word 6 files). If you have both versions, this makes it almost a slam-dunk! What this means is: You can save a Word 6 file on your PC disk at work, bring it home, and Word 6 on your Mac can open it right up. The reverse is also true—in fact you can bop back and forth as much as you want. Even if you don't have the same versions of Word, you can just use the machine with the latest version to save files in the older format (see the illustration on the following page).

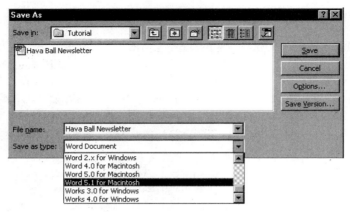

Even if you're not using the same versions of software on the PC and Mac, both platforms let you save to older versions. Here's Word 97 on a PC saving to the older Mac 5.1 file format.

While it's true that PC and Mac **fonts** don't always match up perfectly, and **graphics** aren't always the same on both platforms, taking files across platforms is still a remarkably easy thing to do.

The tricky part is that a PC "knows" a Word file is a Word file because of its three-character extension. When you double-click a file on the PC with a .WRD extension, Windows says to itself, "Ah! This document has a .WRD on the end—I'll launch Word 6 and open it up."

The Mac doesn't care about the filename at all when it tries to figure out what program to open a document with. Instead, when you double-click on a Mac document, the computer looks *inside* the file for the **Creator Code.** This is a four-letter code that serves the same purpose as the three-character extension on a PC. For example, a Mac knows to launch PageMaker when you double-click on a file with the ALD6 code. This Creator Code is also used by the Mac to create the file's distinctive icon. The problem is that files converted from the PC *never have a Creator Code.* Double-clicking on one of these files usually gets you this response:

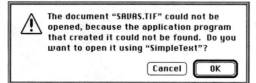

You'll see this if the Mac isn't sure what program created the file. PC files lack the Creator Code the Mac needs to understand what application made the document. PC Exchange can work around this problem.

PC Exchange has this neat ability to **tell your Mac to use three-character extensions** and what programs those extensions should correspond to. This means (if you're a Word 6 user) you can tell your Macintosh that .DOC files should be launched with Word 6 on your Mac.

Here's how to do it for Word. Use this as an example for "mapping" any PC extensions to the corresponding Mac program:

1. Open the **PC Exchange** Control Panel.

2. Click the **Add** button.

3. Enter the DOS Suffix ".DOC" into the **DOS Suffix Box.**

4. **Navigate** to the Microsoft Word 6 application on your hard disk and click once on it.

5. From the **Document Type** drop-down menu, choose an icon that looks like a normal Mac Word file.

6. **Click OK.**

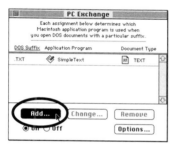
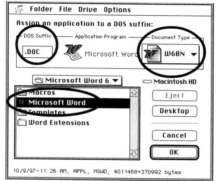

The Add button in PC Exchange lets you map PC three-character filename extensions to specific Mac programs.

Now when you double-click a .DOC document on your Mac, PC Exchange looks at the three-character extension on the file name, automatically launches Word 6 for you, and opens the file.

You don't have to do this. The only reason to configure PC Exchange this way is if you want to **double-click** a PC file from the Finder. Instead, lots of people just launch Word and use the **Open** command within Word to open the file. My favorite method is to just drag the document onto the application (or an alias of the application) that I want the file to open with. Both of these actions tell the Mac to open *that* file with *this* program.

In a nutshell . . .

Here are the four steps to super-easy Windows compatibility:

1. Use a Mac other than a Plus or the MacII.

2. Install the Control Panel **PC Exchange.**

3. Run the same application(s) on your Mac and PC.

4. Optional: Configure PC Exchange to auto-launch PC files.

PC Exchange is not perfect. Mac file names can be as long as 31 characters; Windows 95 users can use a whopping 255 characters in their file names. But PC Exchange still lives in the old DOS world, where the **eight-dot-three** convention is the rule (eight characters, a period, and a three-character extension). This means if you named a document "June Report to Accounting.DOC," PC Exchange will change it to JUNRE~1.DOC.

You can buy more advanced programs that replace PC Exchange in your System Folder and permit longer filenames. One of these programs is called **DOS Mounter 95** ($100, Software Architects). Me? I just live with eight-character filenames and everything works fine.

Okay, So Floppies Work—What About CDs?

The good news is that with PC Exchange and the Extension called **Foreign File Access** your Mac can *read* CDs that have been designed for DOS or Windows. The bad news is you *can't* run game CDs or other interactive titles. To do that, you have to spend some big bucks on additional hardware or software (see "Perfect Compatibility: Running Windows on your Mac," page 256).

So if someone gives you a CD they use in their PC and you want to copy a graphic or spreadsheet from it onto your Mac, great. However, if you run the game "Doom" on your PC at work and you want to take it home and play it on your Mac, you're going to need a lot more than PC Exchange to do it.

Doh! Somebody Gave me a .ZIP file!

Just like us Mac users, PC users have **compression programs** that can reduce the size of some files so you can fit more on a disk. Unfortunately, they don't use the same compression programs we do. You'll know when you've been given a document that's been compressed on a PC when it has a **.ZIP** extension.

To decompress these files, you can use the commercial Mac program **StuffIt Deluxe** ($129, Aladdin Systems) or the shareware program **ZipIt.**

To unzip a file: If someone gives you a PC disk with a "zipped" file, just copy the file to your hard disk and then drag the file's icon on top of ZipIt or StuffIt. This will cause the file to decompress.

Files compressed by the PC standard .ZIP method are easy to decompress with the shareware program ZipIt. Just drag-and-drop!

ZipIt and other great shareware programs are available from user groups and online services. Check out Chapter 13 for more information on these resources.

*Using "zipped" files are way different from using **Zip Disks!** Zip Disks are removable storage products from Iomega. Zip Disks/ Drives have nothing to do with compression— they are just a new type of hard disk.*

Wait a Minute—I Don't Have the Same Program in Both Places!
What if you have WordPerfect at the office and ClarisWorks at home? Maybe you don't want to shell out the big bucks to buy the Mac version of WordPerfect. Are you out of luck? Nope. It's still easy, it just involves one additional step—the file must be **translated.**

Many application programs can convert files. ClarisWorks is a great example of a program that can convert files for you automatically. If you have only ClarisWorks 4 available and somebody gives you an Excel 4 file, all you have to do is use the **Open** command *from within* ClarisWorks, and that Excel file will open right up.

ClarisWorks says to itself, "Hmmm . . . this is not a document in my native format. **Let's see if I can convert it.**" It looks to see if a proper **translator** is installed. Sure enough, inside your System Folder should be a folder called **Claris** that contains translator files.

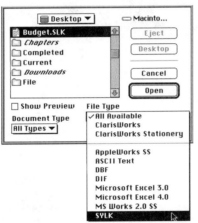

Most major applications contain translators to open files created in other applications.

Microsoft Word has translators also, so you can open WordPerfect, XYWrite, and other commonly created "foreign" document formats.

Here are the standard ways to get a program that can do translations like ClarisWorks, Word, or Excel to open a file that was created in another program:

- **Drag the document icon** onto the application icon you want to use. Or . . .
- **Launch the application** and use the **Open** command to open the file. Or . . .
- **Configure PC Exchange** so that double-clicking the file assigns it to open in the translating program.

Even if Your Application Can't Convert it, Maybe Macintosh Easy Open and MacLink Plus Can

In Chapter Two, I talk about why you should leave the Control Panel **Easy Open** turned off. Yet, for people who frequently transfer files back and forth between a PC and Mac, Easy Open can be a useful little program to have on hand.

Here's what Easy Open is all about: if you double-click on a document that has a Creator Code the Mac doesn't understand (which happens when you have a file created with a program you don't have installed), you normally get an error message.

If Easy Open is installed, **double-clicking on an "unknown" document forces Easy Open to step in and examine it.** It then searches your hard disk to see what programs have the ability to launch it. Finally, Easy Open brings up a list of programs to choose from—you pick which one to use.

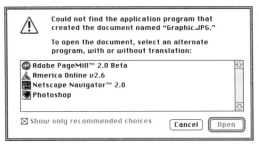

Easy Open is a part of your System software. It will ask you which program to use when opening PC and other unrecognized files.

Why do we care about Easy Open when we can just use PC Exchange to specify launching programs? Simple: Easy Open can work with DataViz's **MacLink Plus** translators, described on the following pages.

MacLink Plus

For many years the folks at DataViz have been working on special translation programs to convert common Mac file formats to PC equivalents and vice-versa. Since 1986 they've been selling these conversion filters and the program that makes them all work together as **MacLink Plus.**

Apple struck a deal with DataViz and started including the MacLink Plus software with System version 7.5. To make it even easier, they made it work with Macintosh Easy Open. If you have the **Easy Open** Control Panel in your Control Panels Folder and **MacLink Plus for Easy Open** Extension in your Extensions Folder, not only will Easy Open ask what program to use to open a file, it will ask you if you want to translate the file into something else.

Here's what I mean: If you double-click on an unknown file with *neither* **Easy Open** *nor* **MacLink Plus** installed, you'll get a message asking if you want to open it with SimpleText, or even a message telling you the Mac can't open the file at all!

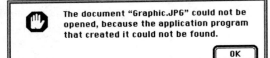

The document "Graphic.JPG" could not be opened, because the application program that created it could not be found.

OK

Without Easy Open or MacLink Plus installed, here's what you might see.

If you double-click on an unknown file with **Easy Open** *only* installed, it will analyze which programs on your hard disk are capable of opening the file, and (if there is more than one) it will prompt you to ask which one to use.

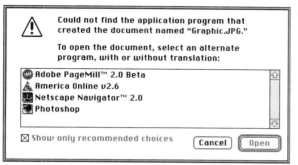

Easy Open knows which programs can open PC files.

If you double-click on an unknown file with *both* **Easy Open and MacLink Plus** installed, Easy Open will give you more options. Easy Open will take into account that MacLink Plus can convert files to other formats.

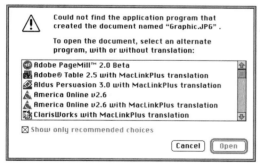

MacLink Plus can translate files so more programs can open them. Easy Open will understand and show you the options.

Perfect Compatibility: Running Windows on Your Mac

Sometimes just being able to understand disks and files isn't enough! Perhaps you need to use an important piece of software that isn't available for the Macintosh. What do you do then?

No problem. You can set up your Mac so that it will **run Windows.**

You have two major choices: either you buy a software emulator that allows your existing Mac hardware to do the job, or you buy some additional hardware to do it.

If You Want to Run Windows (Slowly) Once in a While: Get SoftWindows

SoftWindows is software that lets you run Windows programs on your Macintosh. In Chapter 1 I talked about how the Power Macintosh ROMs contain a program that can **emulate** a 68040 processor. Emulation is a way to trick a program like Word or Excel into thinking it's running on a different type of computer than it actually is.

SoftWindows is a program that runs off your hard drive and **emulates an Intel 80486 chip.** It includes a version of Windows 95 that runs in conjunction with this emulation.

There are two versions of this program available. The most basic version is called **SoftWindows 3.0** from Insignia and costs about $300. It lets you run DOS version 6.22, and Windows 3.1 (the old version of Windows). SoftWindows 95 costs $365 and runs Windows 95. *Soft-Windows 95 is significantly slower* and needs more RAM and disk space than SoftWindows 3.0.

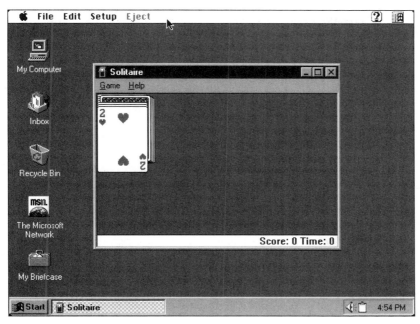

Here's an odd sight—Windows 95 running (slowly) on a Mac!

The **good news** is that SoftWindows is easy to install and requires no additional hardware to make it work—as long as you have at least 16 megabytes of RAM, about 100 megabytes of free disk space, and preferably a Power Mac. In fact, I'm running SoftWindows 95 (glacially) on a PowerBook 5300 right now. SoftWindows also makes your Mac's built-in sound system emulate a SoundBlaster card so that you can actually run PC multimedia and game CDs.

The **bad news** is that SoftWindows ain't cheap, and it's much slower than if you had a real PC. I advise you to consider it only if you have a very fast Power Mac and don't plan to run Windows all the time.

If You Want to Run Windows a Lot: Get a DOS Card

If you took apart your brother-in-law's Windows computer (hey! sounds like fun) you'd find some important items like:

- An Intel 486 or Pentium processor.
- Some RAM.
- A ROM chip (PC folks call it the ROM BIOS).

What if someone put all the same goodies that make one of these non-Mac computers work, soldered them onto a special circuit board, and plugged it into the inside of your Mac? Could you end up with two computers in one? The answer is **yes.**

Several companies (Apple, Reply, and Orange Micro) make boards that do this very thing. Going by names like **DOS Compatibility Card** and **DOS on Mac** cards, they let you use your existing Mac monitor, keyboard, mouse, hard disk, and sometimes RAM, in conjunction with the PC card. **Just hitting a key on your keyboard instantly switches you back and forth** between PC and Mac mode. You can even copy and paste between the two.

Good things about these cards:

- One hybrid Mac takes up less desk space than two computers.
- You can easily transfer data between the two internal systems.
- You can use Apple peripherals like printers, CDs, and modems easily from the PC side as well as the Mac.
- These cards use your Mac's internal sound system for SoundBlaster compatibility.
- Having a PC inside the Mac enhances your PC experience— it allows you to do little things like hit Command E to eject floppies when using the PC.

Bad things about these cards:

- They are a little slower than a regular, separate PC. A plain old PC with the same processor inside will run at least ten percent faster because of a faster data bus.
- They are relatively expensive compared to a regular, separate PC. As of this writing, you can buy one of these cards configured with a 100 MHz Pentium and 16 megabytes of RAM for about $1,200. An entire PC desktop system, including monitor and keyboard, is about the same price.

Special Hybrid Macs from Apple

Apple Computer began selling computers with these DOS cards built-in a few years ago. If you own any of the following, you're already aware of the benefits of having a PC inside your Mac:

- Quadra 610 DOS-Compatible
- Power Mac and Performa 6100 DOS-Compatible
- Macintosh LC 630 DOS-Compatible
- Performa 640 DOS-Compatible
- Power Macintosh 7200/120 DOS-Compatible

Important Things to Consider

The following are some important considerations to take into account before your run out and buy a PC card for your Macintosh.

Where Will You Plug in Your PC card?

First of all, forget trying this with any kind of all-in-one Mac like a Mac Plus, SE, or Classic. They either don't have the kind of slot that can accept these kinds of cards, or they have no slot at all.

Secondly, if this PC-in-a-Mac option sounds attractive, you need to contact the manufacturers of these special cards and tell them what kind of model Mac you have. Then they can tell you if they have a card that will work in your machine and how much it costs.

Here's how to get a hold of these DOS card manufacturers:

Apple Computer: 800-767-2775   www.apple.com
Reply Corporation: 800-955-5295   www.reply.com
Orange Micro: 714-779-2772   www.orangemicro.com

It's very important that you **find out what kind of slot(s)** you have inside your Mac that a PC card could plug into. Here are the three types of slots a Mac can have:

NuBus Slots: Macs that typically have this type of slot are the Mac II series (II, IIci, IIcx, IIfx, etc.). If the card manufacturers say this is the type of slot you would plug the card into, you should be aware that this is the **slowest of the three slots,** and it means that you will get the **least performance** bang for the buck. I would consider buying a separate Windows computer instead.

PDS Slots: Many Performas, Quadras, and Centris Macs have this kind of slot, as do the Power Mac and Performa 6100 series, and they offer good performance.

PCI Slots: Fastest slot type of the three. If you bought your Mac after January 1, 1996, odds are that your Mac has this kind of slot available.

What Processor Does the Card Use?

Depending on where you buy the card, it will have one of three types of processor chips:

- An **Intel 486 chip,** the slowest of the three.
- A **Cyrix 5x86 chip,** a little faster.
- A **Pentium chip,** the fastest.

How Much More RAM Will You Need?

Apple's DOS compatibility cards can use memory on the Mac mother-board. Reply's and Orange Micro's can't. Be aware that you will have to pay for RAM to be installed on these cards.

What Ports do you Have?

Make sure that the card(s) available for your Mac have the ports you need. Things to consider include plugging in a joystick, another monitor, sound in/out, parallel ports, etc.

Extra Tidbits

Just a couple of notes about the two nice features of a Windows machine that you might want or need to emulate on a Mac.

Making Your Menus "Sticky"

Some people like to be able to click on a menu and have it pop open and stay open without having to keep the mouse button down.

Windows does that, and your Mac can do it too. If you've purchased **Now Utilities,** check out the **Now Menus** Control Panel. Just check the "Menus stick when pulled-down" option. If you don't have Now Utilities, get your hands on the shareware program **AutoMenus Pro.** It can do the same thing.

Hey—PCs Have a Two-Button Mouse!

Over the years, PC programs have relied on the right-hand mouse button more and more. Windows 95 makes that button even more important. The best thing to do if you're going to run Windows a lot is to get a two-button mouse like the one made by Kensington (about $60). Otherwise, SoftWindows and the DOS hardware card vendors let you use a key on the keyboard to simulate the right-hand mouse button.

Important Things to Remember

- Working cross-platform between Macs and PCs is easy, as long as you use the right hardware and software tools.

- Almost all Macs can easily understand PC floppy disks— as long as you have a program like PC Exchange installed.

- PC Exchange can also tell PC files what Mac programs should open them, based on their three-character extensions.

- Easy Open and MacLink Plus work together to convert files when you don't have the same programs on both machines.

- SoftWindows is a slow, software-only solution for running Windows on your Mac.

- Three different companies make circuit boards that can "implant" a PC brain inside your Macintosh.

Vendor List

Abbott Systems
62 Mountain Road
Pleasantville, NY 10570
800.552.9157
914.747.4171
fax: 914.747.9115
www.abbottsys.com

Adobe Systems
345 Park Avenue
San Jose, CA 95110.2704
408.536.6000
fax: 408.537.6000
www.adobe.com

Aladdin Systems
165 Westridge Drive
Watsonville, CA 95076.4159
800.732.8881
408.761.6200
fax: 408.761.6206
www.aladdinsys.com

Alsoft
P.O. Box 927
Spring, TX 77383.0927
800.257.6381
713.353.4090
fax: 713.353.9868

America Online
8619 Westwood Ctr. Drive
Vienna, VA 22182.2285
800.827.6364
703.448.8700
fax: 703.448.0760
www.aol.com

Apple Computer
1 Infinite Loop
Cupertino, CA 95014
800.776.2333
408.996.1010
fax: 408.974.6726
www.apple.com

APS Technologies
P.O. Box 4987
6131 Deramus
Kansas City, MO
   64120.0087
800.235.8935
816.483.1600
fax: 816.483.3077
www.apstech.com

**AT&T WorldNet
   Service**
32 Avenue of the Americas
New York, NY 10013.2412
800.242.6005
www.att.com

Berkeley Systems
2095 Rose Street
Berkeley, CA 94709
800.344.5541
510.540.2300
fax: 510.849.9486
www.berksys.com

**BMUG (Berkeley
   Mac Users Group)**
1442A Walnut Street, Suite
   62
Berkeley, CA 94709.1496
800.776.2684 (sales only)
510.549.2684
fax: 510.849.9026
www.bmug.org

Casady & Greene
22734 Portola Drive
Salinas, CA 93908.1119
800.359.4920
408.484.9228
fax: 408.484.9218
www.casadyg.com

CE Software
P.O. Box 65580
1801 Industrial Circle
West Des Moines, IA 50265
800.523.7638
515.221.1801
fax: 515.221.1806
www.cesoft.com

Claris
5201 Patrick Henry Drive
Santa Clara, CA 95052.8168
800.325.2747
408.727.8227
fax: 408.987.3932
www.claris.com

CompuServe
P.O. Box 20212
Columbus, OH 43220
800.848.8199
614.457.8600
fax: 614.457.0348
www.compuserve.com

Connectix
2655 Campus Drive
San Mateo, CA 94403.2520
800.950.5880
415.571.5100
fax: 415.571.5195
www.connectix.com

Corel
The Corel Building
1600 Carling Avenue
Ottawa, ON K1Z 8R7
Canada
800.772.6735
613.728.8200
fax: 613.728.9780
www.corel.com

Dantz Development
4 Orinda Way, Building C
Orinda, CA 94563.9919
510.253.3000
fax: 510.253.9099
www.dantz.com

DataViz
55 Corporate Drive
Trumbill, CT 06611
800.733.0030
203.268.0030
fax: 203.268.4345
www.dataviz.com

Datawatch
234 Ballardvale Street
Wilmington, MA 01887
508.988.9700
fax: 508.988.0697
www.datawatch.com

Deneba Software
7400 SW 87th Avenue
Miami, FL 33173
305.596.5644
fax: 305.273.9069
www.deneba.com

**Diamond
   Communications
   (Supra)**
2880 Junction Avenue
San Jose, CA 95134
800.468.5846
Tech support fax:
   408.325.7171
www.supra.com

DiamondSoft, Inc.
351 Jean Street
Mill Valley, CA 94941
415.381.3303
fax: 415.381.3503
www.fontreserve.com

Digital Chicago
5225 Old Orchard Road,
   Suite 39
Skokie, IL 60077
847.583.8433
www.digitalchi.com

DriveSavers
30-D Pamaron Way
Novato, CA 94949
415.883.4232
800.440.1904
fax: 415.883.0780
www.drivesavers.com

EarthLink Network
3100 New York Drive
Pasadena, CA 91107
818.296.2400
www.earthlink.com

Fractal Design
P.O. Box 66959
Scotts Valley, CA
95067.6959
800.846.0111
408.430.4000
fax: 408.436.9670
www.fractal.com

**Global Village
Communication**
1144 East Arques Avenue
Sunnyvale, CA 94086
800.736.4821
408.523.1000
fax: 408.523.2407
www.globalvillage.com

**IDG Books
Worldwide, Inc.**
919 E. Hillsdale Boulevard,
Suite 400
Foster City, CA 94404
800.434.3422
415.312.0650
www.idgbooks.com

Image Club Graphics
A Division of Adobe
Systems, Inc.
1525 Greenview Drive
Grand Prairie, TX 75050
800.661.9410 (orders)
800.387.9193 (catalog)
fax: 800.814.7783
www.imageclub.com

Insignia Solutions
2200 Lawson Lane
Santa Clara, CA 95054
408.327.6000
fax: 408.327.6105
www.insignia.com

Iomega
1821 W. 4000 S.
Roy, UT 84067
800.456.5522
801.778.1000
fax: 801.778.3748
www.iomega.com

**Kensington
Microware**
2855 Campus Drive
San Mateo, CA 94403
800.535.4242
415.572.2700
fax: 415.572.9675
www.kensington.com

La Cie Limited
8700 SW Creekside Place
Beaverton, OR 97008
503.520.9000
www.lacie.com

MacAddict
Imagine Publishing, Inc.
150 North Hill Drive
Brisbane, CA 94005
888.446.2446
(subscriptions)
415.468.2500
fax: 415.656.2486
www.macaddict.com

Macromedia
600 Townsend Street
San Francisco, CA 94103
800.945.4061
415.252.2000
fax: 415.626.0554
www.macromedia.com

MacUser
950 Tower Lane,
18th Floor
Foster City, CA 94404
800.627.2247
(subscriptions)
415.378.5600 (editorial)
fax: 303.443.5080
www.macuser.com

MacWEEK
50 Beale Street, 14th Floor
San Francisco, CA 94105
609.786.2081
(subscriptions)
415.547.8000 (editorial)
fax: 609.786.2081
(subscriptions)
www.macweek.com

Macworld
501 Second Street
San Francisco, CA 94107
800.288.6848
(subscriptions)
415.243.0505
fax: 415.604.7644
www.macworld.com

**Microsoft
Corportation**
One Microsoft Way
Redmond, WA 98052.6399
800.426.9400
206.882.8080
fax: 206.936.7329
www.microsoft.com

**Netscape
Communications**
501 E. Middlefield. Road
Mountain View, CA 94043
800.NETSITE
415.528.2600
fax: 415.528.4120
www.netscape.com

Now Software
921 SW Washington Street,
Suite 500
Portland, OR 97205.2823
800.237.2078
503.274.2800
fax: 503.274.0670
www.nowsoft.com

Orange Micro
1400 N. Lakeview Avenue
Anaheim, CA 92807
714.779.2772
fax: 714.779.9332
www.orangemicro.com

Peachpit Press
2414 Sixth Street
Berkeley, CA 94710
800.283.9444
510.548.4393
fax: 510.548.5991
www.peachpit.com

Publish
501 Second Street
San Francisco, CA 94107
800.685.3435
(subscriptions)
415.243.0600 (editorial)
fax: 415.495.2354
www.publish.com

Quark
1800 Grant Street
Denver, CO 80203
800.788.7835
303.894.8888
www.quark.com

Radius
215 Moffett Park Drive
Sunnyvale, CA 94089
800.227.2795
408.541.6100
www.radius.com

Reply
4435 Fortran Drive
San Jose, CA 95134
800.801.6898
408.942.4804
fax: 408.942.4897
www.reply.com

Software Architects
19102 N. Creek Parkway,
Suite 101
Bothell, WA 98011.8005
206.487.0122
fax: 206.487.0467
www.softarch.com

Symantec
175 W. Broadway
Eugene, OR 97401
800.441.7234
541.345.3322
fax: 541.334.7400
www.symantec.com

Syncronys Softcorp
3958 Ince Blvd.
Culver City, CA 90232
888.777.5600
213.340.4100
fax: 407.333.9080
www.syncronys.com

Index

screen fonts (same thing), 182
sizes of, 183
what you need with ATM, 183
why created, 185
bitmapped graphics
as tiles, 172
in EPS files, 168
printing, 165
TIFF file format, 168
bits, 30
black-and-white
grayscale, 163
line art, 163
Mac computers, 162
photos, halftoned, 169
Blatner, David, 170
BMUG, 235
company address, 263
phone number for, 236
BMUG Journal, 235
boards. *See* **cards**
bombs. *See* **crashes**
books you should read
and online publications, 243
Apple Internet Connection Kit, 221
BMUG Journal, 235
How to Boss Your Fonts Around, 180
Internet Starter Kit for Macintosh, 221
Macworld Mac Secrets, 244
Real World Scanning and Halftones, 170
Sad Macs, Bombs, and Other Disasters, 107, 244
The Little Mac Book, 104, 180, 195
The Macintosh Bible, 244
Visual QuickStart books, 229
Boomerang. *See* **Super Boomerang**
Bradley, Thomas, 165
brightness
Button Disabler, 53
Screen Control Panel, 59
Broback, Steve, 288
browsers, 222
Home button in, 225
launching, 225
New York font in, 190
bugs, 42
burn in, 49
Button Disabler, 53

C

cables
for printing, 126
SCSI, 38, 112
serial printing, 126
troubleshooting for printing, 128
cache
disk, 78
in Adobe Type Manager, 193
Level Two, 22
Cache Switch, 53
"Calculate folder sizes," 197
Cancel
Escape key, 204
make shortcut with QuicKeys, 136
CanOpener, 97
cards
Apple Serial NB, 53
ATI Video, 59
expansions slots for video cards, 32
PC Card Modem Extension, 62
PC modem c., 62
video, 32
cartridge
using a c. to backup, 100
Casa Blanca Works, 96
Casady & Greene, 70, 93
company address, 263
CDs
AppleCD Audio Player, 65
Audio Volume Extension for sounds, 65
dragging System Folder from, 114
driver, 65
force restart with CD startup disk, 86
Foreign File Access, 65
install CD, 89
mounting with SCSIProbe, 97
playing music, 65
QuickTime Extension, 65
read PC CDs on Mac, 250
startup CDs, 86
why not to drag over items if you've updated, 114
Centris
memory limits for, 24
processors for, 18
CE Software, 134
company address, 263

characters
formatting, 146
invisible, 152
style sheets for, 155
"Character Shapes" in ATM, 193
character styles, 155
checkboxes, 204
Chimes of Doom
bad system software as cause, 113
hardware failure as cause, 113
illustration of Dead Mac, 112
chips
601, 21
603, 603e, 603ev, 21
604, 604e, 21
68000, 18, 20
68020, 18
PMMU for, 22
68030, 18
PMMU is built in, 22
68040, 18, 20
fpu in, 22
PMMU is built in, 22
68LC040, 18
clock speeds of, 21
emulator, 20
graphics accelerator, 59
Intel X86, 18
Pentium, 18
PMMU, 22
PowerPC, 20
PMMU is built in, 22
RAM. *See* RAM
ROM. *See* ROM chips
Chooser
doesn't see printer, 128
printing to more than one printer, 127
circuit boards
plugging in optional circuit boards, 36
CISC, 19
vs. RISC, 21
city-named fonts, 190
built into System software, 198
faster viewing on screen, 198
Claris
company address, 263
Draw, 164
FileMaker, 143
Paint, 163
tech support web address, 239
Works. *See* ClarisWorks

L

Labels Control Panel, 56
  as tool in backup process, 103
La Cie Limited, 96, 264
LAN, MacTCP Control Panel, 60
Landau, Ted, 107, 244
  MacFixIt Web site, 240
"Largest Unused Block," 72, 73
LaserWriter ROM fonts, 191
launch applications
  with QuicKeys, 135
Launcher, 56
LC
  68020 processor, 18
  memory limits for, 24
  VRAM upgrading, 31
Levels command, 171
  how to use it, 172
Level Two cache, 22
LeVitus, Bob, 232
line art
  1-bit, 163
  black-and-white, 163
line screen value, 170
line spacing, preserve in ATM, 193
lines per inch, 170
Link Tool Manager, 54
Litterbox, 288
Little Mac Book, The,
  104, 180, 195
loading order of Extensions, 70
LocalTalk, 126
  Control Panels and Extensions you can disconnect, 64
  if printer is not LT., 128
Location field in browser, 226
locked items, how to trash, 196
lockups
  as a type of crash, 119
  Force Quit application, 202
  why, how to fix, 41
lpi, 170
Lu, Cary, 232

M

MacAddict **magazine,** 233
  company address, 264
Mac Chicago **magazine,** 234
Mac II
  memory limits for, 24
  processors for, 18
  VRAM upgrading, 31
Mac Classic
  memory limits for, 24
  processors for, 18
  ROM on a Mac Classic, 23
Mac FX, processors for, 18
macho software, 142
MacinTalk Extension, 208
Macintosh Performa CD, 86
Macintosh Bible, The, 244
Macintosh Easy Open, 50
Macintosh Guide, 55
MacinTouch Web site, 240
  online articles, 243
MacLinkPlus Setup, 58
Mac OS Easy Open, 51
MacPaint, 162
Mac Plus, 58
  expansion slots, 37
  maximizing memory in, 81
  memory limits for, 24
  processors for, 18
  ROM on a Mac Plus, 23
Macromedia
  company address, 264
  FreeHand, 164
macros, make with QuicKeys, 134
Mac SE
  maximizing memory in, 81
  memory limits for, 24
  processors for, 18
MacTCP, 60, 219, 224
MacTCP Control Panel, 60
Mac user groups
  what are they?, 235
  how to find one near you, 236
  importance of, 235
  Internet support, 221
  sigs, Special Interest Groups, 235
  source for shareware and freeware, 90

MacUser **magazine,** 233
  company address, 264
  helpful in finding a mail-order hard disk company, 118
  online articles, 243
  scooped by *BMUG Journal,* 236
MacWEEK **magazine,** 233
  company address, 264
  helpful in finding a mail-order hard disk company, 118
  online articles, 243
Macworld Mac Secrets, 244
Macworld **magazine,** 67, 233
  company address, 264
  helpful in finding a mail-order hard disk company, 118
  if only one mag, get this one, 244
  online articles, 243
  scooped by *BMUG Journal,* 235
magazines
  Adobe Magazine, 234
  BMUG Journal, 235
  Digital Chicago, 234
    company address, 263, 264
  helpful for finding mail-order hard disk companies, 118
  listen to *Macworld* while driving, 209
  MacAddict, 233
    company address, 264
  MacUser, 39, 118, 233
    company address, 264
  MacWEEK, 118, 233
    company address, 264
  Macworld, 39, 118, 233
    company address, 264
  Publish, 234
    company address, 264
magneto-optical disks
  as backups, 34
mailing lists, 243
  list of mailing lists, 243
maintenance, 99–105
manuals, 144
Map Control Panel, 56
MasterJuggler Pro, 188
McClelland, Deke, 232
megahertz, 21

X

Y

Z

Notes

Three things in human life
are important:
The first is to be kind.
The second is to be kind.
And the third is to be kind.

Henry James

Notes

Show up.
Pay attention.
And speak the truth.

Steve Broback

I live in Woodinville, Washington, with my wife Vicky and our two little ones. When not writing, teaching, or organizing conferences, I love skiing, snorkeling, and most of all spending time with my wife and kids. I bought one of the very first Macs in 1984 and have been using Macintoshes daily ever since.

Robin Williams

I have written over a dozen books, mostly Macintosh or design/ typography related, that have been translated into all sorts of weird languages. I live in Santa Fe, New Mexico, on a rise overlooking miles of short, stubby trees that don't get in the way of the sunset. I'm still a single mom of three kids, but they're growing up. For more info about me than you'd ever care to know, go to ratz.com.

Other books by Robin:
The Little Mac Book
  (four editions)
The Mac is not a typewriter
Beyond The Mac is not
  a typewriter
The PC is not a typewriter
PageMaker 4, Mac
PageMaker 4, Windows
PageMaker 5 Companion,
  Mac
Tabs and Indents
  on the Macintosh
Jargon, an informal
  dictionary of
  computer terms
How to Boss Your Fonts
  Around
A Blip in the continuum
Home Sweet Home Page
The Non-Designer's
  Design Book
The Non-Designer's
  Web Book (summer,
  1997)

This Book

This book was created in PageMaker 6.5. I love PageMaker. It's silly to create a book in anything except PageMaker. Typefaces used are the Antique Olive family for the heads, Garamond for the body copy (both from Adobe), and Litterbox by Dean Stanton (from Image Club Graphics) for the front pages and quotes.

The delightful clip art is by Dean Stanton, from the Hoopla Collection, available from Image Club Graphics. Thanks ever so much, Dean! You're great.